What, When, & How to
Talk to Students
About Alcohol
&
Other Drugs

A Guide for Teachers

What, When, & How to Talk to Students About Alcohol & Other Drugs

A Guide for Teachers

Gail Gleason Milgram, Ed. D.
Thomas Griffin, M.S.W.

Hazelden

First published January, 1986.

Copyright © 1986, Hazelden Foundation.
All rights reserved. No portion of this publication
may be reproduced in any manner without the written
permission of the publisher.

ISBN: 0-89486-336-3

Printed in the United States of America.

Editor's Note:
    Hazelden Educational Materials offers a variety of information on chemical dependency and related areas. Our publications do not necessarily represent Hazelden or its programs, nor do they officially speak for any Twelve Step organization.

To

Lynn and Anne
Jennifer and Jeffrey

ACKNOWLEDGMENTS

A special note of thanks to Linda Allen for her organization and coordination of all aspects of the manuscript, and to Janet O'Connor for her excellent manuscript typing. We also wish to thank the following for their kind permission to quote from works held in copyright:

T. Griffin and R. Svendsen. *The Student Assistance Program: How It Works*. Center City, MN, Hazelden Foundation, 1980.

T. Griffin, R. Svendsen, and D. McIntyre. *Chemical Health, School Athletes and Fine Arts Activities*. Center City, MN, Hazelden Foundation, 1984.

R. R. Lingeman. *Drugs from A to Z: A Dictionary*. New York, McGraw-Hill Book Co., 1974.

G. Milgram. *What, When, and How to Talk to Children About Alcohol and Other Drugs: A Guide for Parents*. Center City, MN, Hazelden Foundation, 1983.

CONTENTS

INTRODUCTION

What, When, and How to Talk to Students About Alcohol and Other Drugs: A Guide for Teachers is written for educators challenged by new demands, new health concerns, and an increasingly complex set of expectations for education. The schools today are often very different from those we attended as children. Educators are being asked to play an increasingly important role in the development of their students. We are expected to expand our curriculum to include health issues and social concerns including death and dying, eating disorders, child and sexual abuse, teen suicide, chemical use, and the changing family system. Educators are often asked to take action on new and complex issues without prior experience or training.

Talking to students about alcohol and other drugs is a task facing all educators today. *Student Drug Use, Attitudes and Beliefs 1975 -1982,*[1] indicates that approximately 70% of all seniors in high school drank alcohol on a monthly basis, 59% have smoked marijuana, and over 90% have experimented with alcohol before graduation. The *Sixteenth Annual Gallup Poll of the Public's Attitude Toward the Public Schools*[2] conducted for Phi Delta Kappa in 1984, found that over 80% of all Americans believe alcohol and other drug abuse should be required subject matter for all students. Clearly, educators are being challenged to talk to students knowledgeably and persuasively about the serious public health topic of chemical use.

Many of us have not been adequately prepared through teacher preparation programs to discuss the complex issues surrounding chemical use and nonuse with students. Only in the past decade have colleges and universities included course

1

work on alcohol and other drugs, and then often as only a small portion of other course offerings. Many of us have attended seminars, workshops, and lectures on chemical dependency and related issues. School districts throughout the country are developing policies, procedures, and curriculum guides to respond to the problems of student chemical use. Yet it is often not clear what, when, and how to talk to students about alcohol and other drugs. The purpose of this book is to offer information, ideas, and encouragement to teachers who want to take an active role in preventing and identifying chemical use problems of students.

Many teachers are also parents and share the experience of all of those parents who grew up in another era. Although it is true that parents through the ages have shared similar concerns for the health and well-being of their children, many elements of present times are dramatically different from when we were growing up. Simple answers from adults about the way things used to be often stimulate anger, and are interpreted by children as a lack of understanding of today's world and the significance of today's problems. This does not imply that children have not responded negatively to parents' comments before the 1980s. It does reinforce the concept that some elements of the present society pose more of a threat in our children's world than they did to us when we were children.

Fear of nuclear war or accident, threats to the natural environment, lack of opportunity for meaningful contributions to society through work, and a sense of rapid societal change all create a stressful life situation for students today. They are answering complex questions about life that were not a part of our growing up. Most teachers and parents are genuinely concerned about the best ways to help young people cope with stress and provide support for developing a healthy lifestyle. It is our hope that this book will help teachers talk more clearly and effectively with students about the very important lifestyle decisions regarding chemical use.

Teachers are not alone in their efforts to prevent these problems. Society is beginning to take a very aggressive approach to responding to alcohol and other drug problems, especially among youth. Efforts to raise the minimum age for purchasing alcohol to 21 years are under way in every state. Some states require schools to offer instruction and/or counseling services about chemical use. Mothers Against Drunk Drivers (MADD) and Students Against Driving Drunk (SADD) chapters are active and developing in many locations throughout the country. These citizen groups are encouraging legislative and judicial action to reduce the risks presented to all of us by drunk driving.

Students and adults are clearly stating a sense of concern and outrage over the preventable problem of drinking and driving. Community groups organized through civic organizations, churches, synagogues, and governmental agencies are planning and implementing community-based prevention efforts. Hospitals, treatment centers, and government programs offer a wide range of outpatient counseling, detoxification, and residential rehabilitation services for adolescents as well as adults. Each of us has a role and responsibility to help young people learn about alcohol and other drug issues so they can make safe and healthy decisions about the use or nonuse of any chemical.

This book is organized into five sections. Information on the societal use of alcohol and other drugs and the impact on the affected person and the family are presented in Part I. Youthful alcohol and other drug use in relation to family and peers is also explored, and patterns and reasons for use are discussed. This section also discusses community attitudes toward alcohol and other drug education and examines the role of the school in this area.

Various experiences of childhood and adolescence, provided in Part II, are also necessary to provide a perspective of the adolescent reality and to suggest topics relevant to the needs of children of all ages. One discussion with a ten-year-old on alcohol does not answer the questions that the same person has at sixteen. The communication process must be an ongoing one focusing on the experiences and situations of the student's age. The relationship and significance of the peer group are also discussed. Alcohol and other drug information is presented according to grade level. Spontaneous and planned activities are also presented by grade level. Goals for health promotion, prevention, and assistance are detailed since goal structure provides the basis for program design and implementation. A chart outlining student outcomes in self-awareness, social skills, social systems, and chemical use in American society concludes Part II.

The third section of this book is really the "how to" part. It is composed of policy and program elements which provide the framework for incorporating alcohol and other drugs into the school's policies, curriculum, and services. The necessary items are provided in checklist form with the recommendation that a time line for completion be established to assure implementation. Also provided are communication techniques, discussion exercises, and other strategies to examine personal attitudes and provide a beginning for teachers and students to talk about alcohol and other drugs. These are offered as door openers and can be modified to suit various classroom experiences. Hopefully, they will enable open and honest communication about alcohol and other drugs to become an accepted and spontaneous part of discussions. A plus is that students will feel free to seek information and guidance on other sensitive topics.

Part IV of the text will enable teachers to identify a student with alcohol or other drug problems, understand that help is available, and present techniques for finding help. School policies, student assistance programs, and employee assistance programs are also discussed in this section. A brief summary statement concludes the text in Part V.

Two appendixes are also included. Appendix A presents necessary content information on alcohol and other drugs.

This background information is important because many adults in our society have never received objective and honest information on alcohol and other drugs. It also enables teachers to be comfortable in discussing the topic and say, "I don't know," if this is the honest response. Appendix B discusses chemical dependency. It clarifies what is often bewildering to us, and provides understanding of the impact of addiction on the affected person, the family, and the school.

Resources for additional information are also provided so that interested teachers and parents may explore the wealth of available resources and materials.

PART I: WHAT
Societal Use of Alcohol and Other Drugs

Although many people don't think about it and may not even be aware of it, alcohol is a drug. It is a depressant which acts on the central nervous system. Because alcohol is a socially acceptable, legal beverage and is frequently served for a variety of reasons, many people don't consider it a drug. We also don't think about and are unaware of other drugs we take. Some of these are over-the-counter medicines and others are prescription drugs. We often take one or more of these drugs and drink alcohol in the same day.

The problem with our taking medications is that we often don't think about it, and we don't think about taking a drink either. This doesn't mean every time we do this it's harmful or risky. However, it sets the stage for what society teaches our young and what we are comfortable discussing. Unfortunately, most of us haven't received enough information to be aware of and be comfortable with our own drug use or to enable us to share information with students. If you feel you'd like to have some basic information on alcohol and other drugs before we begin, please turn to Appendix A.

We are a drug using society. Approximately 70% of our population drinks alcoholic beverages during the year. Since over-the-counter medications, prescribed medications, and common stimulants (caffeine and nicotine) are included in the discussion of drugs and drug-taking, it is difficult to estimate the small percentage of the population that has not taken any drugs in the previous year.

Our reliance on taking substances is an unconscious outgrowth of feelings about what it means to use drugs, and our attitude toward comfort and discomfort. First, let's discuss the difficulties in defining who is a drug user. This is also a problem related to attitudes. If you ask a person if he or she is a drinker or nondrinker, the following often occurs. The person responds to the question as though you had said "problem drinker" or "alcoholic." It is also possible that people only think of the meaning of the word in terms of quantity ("Do I drink a lot?"), frequency ("Do I drink often?"), reasons ("Do I drink for the wrong reasons?"), and consequences ("Does my drinking cause problems?"). Since the majority of people in our society could and would answer no to the above questions, many of them will respond that they are not drinkers.

Another element that further confuses us is our lack of knowledge of the alcohol content in twelve ounces of beer, five ounces of wine, and one and one-half ounces of distilled spirits. If we incorrectly think any of these alcoholic beverages contain less alcohol than the other, then our definition of drinking may revolve around only those people who consume distilled spirits rather than all who consume beverage alcohol. For our purposes, a drinker is defined as a person who consumes *any* alcoholic beverage during the year; this consumption may even be a small quantity on a rare or occasional basis for appropriate reasons.

Secondly, we need to think about our attitude toward comfort and discomfort and how this relates to drugs. Being comfortable is considered good, and things that impede our comfort should be eliminated. In other words, it is not okay to be uncomfortable in our society. If we are not comfortable, or not feeling 100%, we can take some kind of drug and quite often we do. We go to our pockets, desk drawers, the friend down the hall, or our medicine cabinets to get something to ease our headache, muscle soreness, neuritis, neuralgia, cold symptoms, indigestion, tension, etc.

Taking medicine for discomfort may be an appropriate response to the situation. However, the real issue is: Is the taking of a drug a conscious decision, or is it an automatic response? Are we thinking about our use of various chemicals in the context of drugs? Are we aware of why we are taking something? Are we happy with the message given by this behavior, that it is okay to take something to alleviate discomfort and problems? The need for thoughtful examination and clarification is necessary if we are to have an honest framework for discussing drug-related issues with students.

Youthful Alcohol and Other Drug Use

Alcohol and other drugs are part of American society. We adults use alcohol and other drugs and young people learn from us. They are aware of what we use, how we use, and for what reasons. In fact, adults as parents are usually the first to introduce children to alcohol and other drugs. When drugs are introduced, there should be discussion about what it is, why it's being used, how the people feel about its use, and what problems, if any, are associated with its use. Too often young children watch adults have a drink or take a drug without ever talking about these things. It is as if society has decided the young don't understand, don't have any questions, or don't need to know. The message that it's not something to talk about often comes through loud and clear.

Since most young people are introduced to alcohol and other drugs at home, a pattern of drug-taking behavior has been established. Norms are set for this behavior; however, these norms are usually not stated or discussed. The adolescent peer group, often blamed as the cause of adolescent drug use, is usually not responsible for the introduction to alcohol and other drugs. However, the peer group is often responsible for activities that allow continued use. This is understandable since adolescents are at a stage of life when they are desperately trying to become independent and establish their own norms of behavior. This is the key to our concern.

Patterns of adolescent alcohol and other drug use are presented in descriptive studies of adolescent behaviors. A recent nationwide study of alcohol use, conducted in 1980, found that 73% of the sixteen- to eighteen-year-olds surveyed are drinkers.[3] Another nationwide study conducted in 1978, found that 87% of the high school population (grades ten to twelve) had at least tried alcohol; 77% of males and 73% of females were current users.[4] These percentages have not changed dramatically over time. A study conducted of New York state high school students in 1962 found 81% of the males and 66% of the females identified as drinkers; a study of high school students in Oregon in 1967-68 found 88% of the males and 84% of the females identified as drinkers; and a study of California students in grades seven to twelve in 1975 identified 82% of the males and 80% of the females as drinkers.[5] Clearly, alcohol use has been a part of adolescent behavior for years. This doesn't mean it is without risk or that it doesn't need to be discussed. A significant reason for concern is the fact that intoxication is often considered acceptable, and this creates a serious risk to our youth.

Reasons for adolescent alcohol use are similar to our reasons for drinking: to relax, be social, and have a good time. However, some adolescents drink to get intoxicated. Approximately 30% of the young people surveyed in 1978 responded that they were intoxicated six or more times in the last year.[6] A Minnesota survey[7] conducted in 1983 found 46% of all Minnesota high school seniors reported drinking five or more drinks in one sitting at least once during the two-week period before completing the survey form. Though most adolescents outgrow this stage, it does represent a significant risk to the person and others.

Getting high, or modifying one's mood with a chemical, is not limited to alcohol. The 1983 Minnesota survey[8] discovered that 61% of all high school seniors reported driving after drinking. Other drugs pose their own set of problems. Though the risk of intoxication may also be present, there are additional risk factors related to the type of drug obtained. The drug may not be what is expected, it may be stronger, and there may be other dangers and consequences from taking the drug. Reasons for most other drug use by adolescents also mirror adult society: to relax and modify moods.

A 1982 study of high school seniors[9] found the following:

	Used	Used in Past Month
Marijuana	59.0%	29.0%
LSD	9.6%	2.4%
Cocaine	16.0%	5.0%
Heroin	11.0%	2.0%
Amphetamines	36.0%	14.0%
Quaaludes/Barbiturates	15.0%	3.0%
Tranquilizers	14.0%	2.0%
Cigarettes	74.0%	34.4%
Alcohol	93.0%	70.0%
PCP	6.0%	1.0%
Inhalants	18.0%	3.0%

A 1978 study of adolescents in New Jersey[10] found that rates of alcohol and other drug use appear to be grade related. Judith Green's 1979 overview of drug use[11] also reported use of licit and illicit drugs increases with age during adolescent years. She also found that the sex-related patterns of drug use during high school and young adult years seem to be disappearing. However, Richards notes that higher proportions of males than females were involved in heavy drug use, though nearly equal proportions of males and females reported some illicit use of drugs.[12]

These statistics clearly demonstrate that there is a wide variety of drugs available to our adolescent population. They point out that many young people try licit and illicit drugs. They also demonstrate that, in many cases, experimenters do not continue to use the drug. And the statistics identify a group of young people who are taking drugs on a regular basis.

In addition, statistics help us become aware that some adolescents experience problems as a result of their chemical use. Some drive after drinking alcohol; some demonstrate poor judgment as a result of use, which results in failing grades, problems with family and friends; and some get physically hurt.

Community Attitudes Toward Alcohol and Other Drug Education

Development of school programs to prevent alcohol and other drug problems of students must reflect the standards, norms, and beliefs of each community. Each community is faced with the challenge of providing quality education for young people. Decisions about chemical use are critical issues in the lives of young people. It is necessary for all those responsible for their education to cooperate in providing guidance toward responsible and healthy decisions regarding chemical use and nonuse.

Parents, teachers, counselors, law enforcement officials, and other concerned citizens in every community realize, to some degree, the serious problems that result from alcohol and other drug use by young people. However, there is often confusion, uncertainty, and disagreement about the best ways to resolve these problems. The concept of chemical health is a new, positive, and comprehensive response to chemical use issues and problems. Chemical health contributes to general health and is defined as a state of spiritual, physical, emotional, and social well-being which results in responsible decisions about chemical use and nonuse.

Chemical health recognizes that people experience a variety of harmful consequences as a result of the inappropriate use of mood-altering drugs, one of which is dependency or addiction. Chemical use problems are defined as physical, emotional, social, or spiritual problems resulting directly from a person's use of chemicals or indirectly from a family member's or other's use of chemicals. In order to develop school programs that will be accepted by the community and school, it is important to consider a few key factors.

1. Are curriculum goals and teaching strategies carefully designed and based on current knowledge about effective health education approaches?

Teachers and school administrators will be able to present curriculum to parents in a confident and professional manner if they are aware of past prevention research results and are knowledgeable about current trends and theories of prevention. Parents will be more likely to support school efforts and offer information and ideas to their children at home that are consistent with the school's prevention messages. If parents understand curriculum goals and content and believe school staff are aware of current knowledge and strategies, the community will feel more hopeful and optimistic.

2. Is the school district board and administration willing to commit adequate time, personnel, and material resources?

Despite the clear risks chemical use problems present to the health and longevity of young people, school boards and administrators are sometimes reluctant to rearrange schedules, staff responsibility, and budget items necessary to develop and implement certain types of prevention efforts. In planning program efforts, it is imperative to involve

school district decision makers so they will support the
program by allocating sufficient staff time and resources.
3. *How willing, interested, and prepared are teachers to
   implement prevention curriculum?*
Many teachers have had little or no training in talking to
students about alcohol and other drugs. Most teachers
recognize the problems students experience with chemicals
and want to help reduce those problems. Yet many teachers
do not feel prepared to address the complexity and enor-
mity of the issues surrounding chemical health. The process
of program development must include teacher training
opportunities to help teachers better understand their roles,
responsibilities, and limitations. The teachers must also be
invited and encouraged to participate in the program
planning process.
4. *What are the specific needs and interests of students?*
National research has consistently shown similar attitudes
and patterns of chemical use throughout the country.
However, regional variations occur as well as differences
among cultural and ethnic groups, school size, and religious affiliation. Student input through survey research and
participation of students on planning groups will help
develop programs relevant to the needs, interests, and life
experiences of the young people in any community. Past
program efforts in related topics, strength of already
existing peer-led student programs, and the influence of
other institutions within the community may all impact on
the acceptance and outcome of prevention efforts. Learning
about the unique characteristics of the student body will
help improve effectiveness of prevention efforts.
5. *Are parents supportive of school-based health programs?*
Most parents agree alcohol and other drug problems exist
and present a health risk to young people today. Not all
parents agree as to the best ways to approach these problems and reduce risks. Some parents strongly believe the

school is the best place to discuss decisions about alcohol and other drug use. Others believe these discussions are the responsibility and right of the family. In developing and implementing school programs, parental input can provide direction and support while reducing the likelihood of community criticism of future program efforts. We all have a role to play in the prevention of chemical use problems. The more we can openly discuss those roles, the greater the likelihood our efforts will be complementary and successful.

Attention to these five factors will increase the acceptance of prevention curriculum within a community and increase the degree of cooperation between family and school. In reality, all attitudes and rules, explicit or implied, that govern schools and communities will impact on program development and should be considered by planners.

Role of the School

As a society, we are interested in education and prevention of problems. In fact, our belief system motivates us to assume schools can and should handle problems of society. Though in many situations schools need to play a significant role, the responses often are that they shouldn't be the "dumping ground" to correct all of society's ills. Instead many assume others should be responsible for education in certain areas, and schools can't be expected to fit everything into their curriculum. The educational system does have a point; our expectations of what the schools need to do is very high. However, some significant issues need to be incorporated into the school system due to the great potential for impact that lies with our educators, the number of people involved, and also because the schools house the population requiring the information.

The school is uniquely qualified to incorporate alcohol and other drug education into its curriculum. The most significant reason for this is the educators; they are trained to teach, able to direct discussions, and possess the skills and abilities necessary to interact with the young. The school also takes on an important role in the life of students. As they grow and develop, the school's environment is significant; educational tasks are key elements in growth from childhood to adolescence to adult status. The school also provides the opportunity for students of the same age level to interact. This factor adds a positive dimension to the young person's perspective of school. Though students may anxiously await holidays and vacations, they get restless after a while as the structure and interaction with friends are missed.

The role of the school in prevention and response to drug use and problems is not a choice of action or inaction, but rather a choice of acting purposefully and systematically or sporadically and inconsistently.

What does this mean for the school, the teacher, the principal? What should schools do to respond to chemical health issues and problems? Historically, law enforcement agencies and schools have been designated responsible for reducing the supply of illegal chemicals, monitoring distribution of legal chemicals, and reducing demand for these chemicals through education. The schools today are being asked to take an increasingly active role in both identifying students' chemical use problems and preventing those problems through education.

What can schools realistically be expected to accomplish in these areas? Efforts to respond effectively to alcohol and other drug issues and problems in our communities can be considered in many ways. One way to conceptualize a comprehensive effort is to view all of our efforts as part of a whole. The following chart[13] is an example.

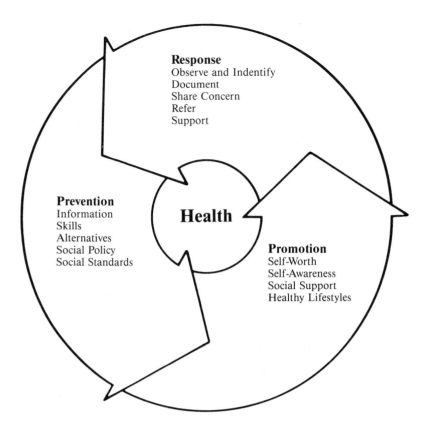

Goals for Health Promotion, Prevention, and Assistance

Establishment of goals provides the basis for program design and implementation. It is a necessary first step in alcohol and other drug education efforts. Three areas detailed in this section are health promotion, prevention, and response to problems. Though these are presented separately, they are related to each other and provide a comprehensive structure for education efforts.

Health promotion is the most general and focuses on healthy development of people rather than responses to specific problems and concerns. Health promotion is a

17

process in which each person's self-worth is acknowledged and nurtured, while personal and social support are developed and strengthened. Health promotion efforts can be integrated easily into ongoing curriculum and activities of most schools and can form the cornerstone of a chemical health program. Examples of health promotion efforts are:

1. Efforts to acknowledge and nurture each person's self-worth separate from performance in an activity.
2. Programs to increase self-awareness among students and understand the variety of feelings or emotions experienced.
3. Efforts to develop personal, social, and spiritual support systems, including strong peer support.
4. Activities that focus on healthy lifestyles, including lifetime sports, good nutrition, and stress management.

Prevention is directed toward those people who do not have problems with alcohol or other drugs. The goals of prevention efforts are:

1. To reduce the likelihood that young people will become involved in illegal and inappropriate drug use or develop chemical use problems such as poor performance in school, family disruption, drunken driving, alcohol-related damage to the unborn, and chemical dependency.
2. The development of clear norms regarding the appropriate use and nonuse of alcohol and other drugs.

There are several categories of prevention efforts essential to the goals of chemical health.

A. Programs that provide important information young people need to make healthy decisions about chemical use and nonuse. While information alone is not likely to prevent problems, it is an important part of a prevention effort.
B. Efforts to develop essential social skills people need in order to make healthy and appropriate decisions regarding alcohol and other drugs.
C. Activities that help people establish and maintain healthy and nonchemical alternative pursuits. These

activities range from lifetime sports to nonchemical parties following school events.

D. Social policy measures such as school policies on the use of alcohol and other drugs, drunk driving laws, and other regulations related to drugs that help people understand the consequences of inappropriate behaviors.

E. Efforts to establish appropriate standards for use and nonuse within families, social institutions, and the community. School athletics and fine arts programs can provide unique opportunities to enlist the cooperation and support of parents and students in reducing chemical use among students.

Response involves providing assistance to people and families experiencing chemical use problems. The process of responding to problems within the school includes several steps.

1. Observing and identifying educational behaviors of concern.
2. Documenting specific behaviors of concern.
3. Sharing concerns with the student by a concerned staff member.
4. If appropriate, referring for assistance, which may or may not include a diagnostic evaluation for chemical dependency or some other problem.
5. For those who undergo treatment or therapy, providing aftercare support upon return to their community.

While professionals within some schools are involved in the diagnosis of chemical dependency and the provision of chemical dependency treatment or therapy, most schools rely on community resources to provide these services. The primary role of the school in the broad area of response to student alcohol or other drug problems is usually twofold.

* Having a process and procedure for identifying and responding to chemical use problems among students; and

* Providing support to the chemically dependent student during treatment and afterward, and to those students who are affected indirectly by a family member or other's use of chemicals.

Because of their unique patterns, coaches and activity directors can observe student behaviors that may not be apparent to other school staff. It is essential that the procedures established by coaches and activity directors for identifying and responding to chemical use problems among student activity participants be consistent with those in place for all students within the regular school day.

While the school has a significant role in each component of the chemical health model, it must be careful not to assume total responsibility. Schools can organize an advisory group to be responsible for assessing program needs, planning appropriate program efforts, and assisting in evaluating the impact of these efforts. It is important that this group involve parents, students, and professionals from the community as well as school staff in order to coordinate school efforts with other programs and existing needs and resources in the community. The group must also identify those services and programs which are consistent with the purpose and budget capacity of the school.

The school can be an effective and integral component of a community response to chemical use problems. The challenge to school staff is to determine the needs of the schools, the resources available, and then plan a comprehensive, purposeful, and systematic program which will best serve students in the community. Schools cannot be expected to do the job alone; but in cooperating with other components of the community the school can respond to student problems, provide instruction designed to prevent student problems, and create an environment which will promote the health of all students.

Summary

The WHAT is discussion about alcohol and other drug use with students. It is information, attitudes, and beliefs. Educators do not have to be drug experts to discuss use of and feelings about alcohol and other drugs. However, they do have to be honest and deal with the reality of the students. It must be realized that the students' information on alcohol and other drugs may be vague, they may be unsure of how they feel about drug use, and they may not have had the opportunity to discuss issues related to drugs.

Community attitudes toward alcohol and other drug education need to be assessed and understood as the community provides the support for program development and implementation. The role of the school in prevention and education is significant, since the school provides a safe and open atmosphere for discussion of these issues. Teachers are also skilled in working with students and offer the key to program success.

PART II: WHEN

When to talk to students about alcohol and other drugs must be rooted in the reality of their world, as well as ours. What are their needs at a particular time? What are they observing that needs to be clarified? And what direct experiences are they having? This requires our being honest about what they have already learned, our own feelings about alcohol and other drugs, and our willingness to discuss these topics. It might also require overcoming an earlier message from our family or society that there's nothing to talk about. Whether the situation is spontaneous or planned will depend on a variety of factors, including the age of the child and his or her needs and interests.

Age of Students: Needs and Interests

Each person, regardless of age, has basic human needs. Developmental Psychologist Abraham Maslow characterizes these needs as: physiological needs, safety and security needs, the need for love and belonging, esteem needs, and the need for self-actualization.[14]

Physiological needs are the basic human requirements for food, oxygen, water, and sleep; safety and security needs are clothing, shelter, and protection from the environment. The need for love and belonging includes family and friends. Esteem needs include a feeling of self-worth, feeling good about one's activities and/or career. The need for self-actualizing is the need to do what one is capable of doing.

To reach the level of self-actualization, the other needs have to be met. It is also important that we understand all of these needs because the actions people choose to fulfill them are important in growth and development. They are also related to drug-taking behaviors, since drugs are one method people may use to attempt to fill a need, such as belonging or to mask the unfulfillment of a need.

When we look at children in terms of needs, their physical needs are clearly perceptible. Children from birth through adolescence and young adulthood need to eat, satisfy their thirst, breathe, and sleep. They get cranky when they're hungry, thirsty, or tired. The same can be said for adults. In most cases, these needs are easily satisfied by eating, drinking, or sleeping. Safety and protection needs for clothing, shelter, and protection from hostile environments are somewhat more complex. Clothing and shelter may be simple enough to understand and provide; however, security is more than this. It is stability and consistency in the home. Guidelines for behavior need to be established, understood, and respected. Of course, this doesn't mean that rules are made never to be changed. However, it does mean that rules are enforced until such time as they are changed. This is an extremely important point. Children and adolescents need to know what are accepted behaviors, what behaviors are unacceptable, and what the consequences of inappropriate behavior will be. This establishes a secure framework in which the child or adolescent can function. It also allows infractions of the rules to be dealt with in a predetermined and consistent manner with the school and community's philosophy.

The need for love and belonging occurs first within the child's family. This enables the child to grow, making mistakes at times, with the knowledge that love is not withdrawn. As the child grows, the need for love and belonging is enlarged to include friends for companionship and acceptance. Rejection by the group is very painful to children and even more so to adolescents. Adolescents need their friends for reinforcement of who they are; the group becomes the means to personal acceptance as well as group satisfaction. Though this implies the group has powers, and in many ways it does, it does not mean the person only has group values and not personal ones. It is also important to remember that groups of adolescents often form due to mutual likes and interests (sports, hobbies, and other activities). When we realize love and belonging needs are also met by friends, it should enable us to view the group in a positive way. They may all dress alike, act alike, and seem to be carbon copies of each other because of the need to be accepted.

The adolescent peer group is most often an untapped resource for teachers. For too long we have viewed peer pressure as a negative influence on children's behavior. We need to recognize that young people can be a powerful, positive influence on each other. Peer-led health education programs have already demonstrated the capability of delaying young adolescents from smoking cigarettes. Current research efforts are underway to apply this same positive peer model to decisions about alcohol and other drug use.

In many ways, parents and teachers are apprehensive of the adolescent peer group. We may be somewhat threatened because the group seems to be more important in the life of adolescents than we are as adults. But we all know that this normal process of growth and development includes pulling away from family and other adult input. We often incorrectly decide that adolescents don't need or want to talk with adults because they have their friends. Although the adolescent peer group discusses many issues, all of the important and relevant topics are often not discussed. The classroom can be an ideal environment to encourage young people to openly and honestly discuss serious health issues and decisions. The educator is in a position to create an environment which allows students to feel comfortable and safe in considering decisions about alcohol and other drug use. Social pressure to use chemicals is clearly one of the major reasons for adolescent chemical use. It is imperative that we, as educators, learn to create an environment in which positive peer pressure will encourage delaying the use of alcohol and other drugs, help the student recognize the risks of excessive use of any chemical, and stimulate discussion of acceptable alternatives for high-risk situations (driving under the influence, riding with an impaired driver).

Esteem needs are also critical through all phases of growth and development. A feeling of personal worth is necessary for each of us every day. Yet our self-esteem is challenged regularly by comments from family and friends. These comments may or may not be intended to diminish self-esteem but often result in our not feeling too good about ourselves. As children grow, we often walk a fine line between helping them understand right and wrong while still making them feel good about themselves and their abilities. If a child's or adolescent's self-esteem is shaky, his or her positive aspects should be stressed. The child should be motivated to do something that will help rebuild his or her self-image. Since drugs are often society's answer to not feeling good about one's self, self-esteem is critical. Drugs may be seen by some as an answer to feeling unworthy or down on oneself. However, when the answer is not found, the person may continue to take the drug for the temporary good received or may become dependent on the drug and thus increase his or her problems.

The need for self-actualization is the need to feel fulfilled or to do what we are able to do. Unfortunately, people cannot be self-actualizing if their other basic needs are not met. That is, if we are hungry, or feel unloved, or have low self-esteem, it is impossible for us to achieve at our highest possible levels. Self-actualization may also be hindered by other things (financial conditions) and create tremendous frustration in people. Frustration is often a part of our everyday lives and the lives of our students. Coping techniques are often developed to deal with unmet needs. Some of us clean a closet or a room to provide a sense of satisfaction, others jog, many listen to music, some withdraw to a quiet place, still others shop. Visiting friends, taking on a new project, reading a book may all be devices used to regain our equilibrium or sense of self. Some people may choose to take a drug to cope with unmet needs and might, therefore, complicate the situation. Discussing appropriate ways of coping with frustration is an important part of communicating about alcohol and other drugs.

To discuss the needs and interests of students concerning alcohol and other drugs requires a framework. The one we have chosen is using periods of growth and development as they're defined by the educational system. Though schools throughout the country have different ways of dividing children by age, they're similar enough to allow us to use this system. It will also help us identify the needs and interests of our young people and their peer group, not relying solely on chronological age. Our discussion will focus on the following periods of life:

preschool............................birth to five years
elementary school (kindergarten
    through sixth grade) ....five to twelve years
upper elementary or junior high (grades
    seven through nine).............thirteen to fifteen years
high school (grades ten
    through twelve)...............sixteen to eighteen years

The preschool years are extremely important in the child's growth and development. Much is learned at this time, and many of the learnings are direct and extremely visible (walking, talking, etc.). The indirect learnings are not as perceptible and visible (thinking processes, effects from experiences, etc.). Both the direct and the indirect learnings regarding alcohol and other drugs need to be considered. Children at this stage may be aware that their parents have a beverage that they're not allowed to drink or have been given only a sip. They may have seen parents acting differently and may have connected the different behavior to something that has been consumed. And they may have heard parents or others discussing someone's drinking. Children may also have watched their parents or older siblings take medication to get well or feel better, and they may have been given medicine themselves. In fact, the doctor-perscription-and-feeling-better-syndrome may be strongly implanted in their minds.

The most important element for this stage is that it's okay to ask questions about alcohol and other drugs, and that an attempt will be made to answer these questions. We often spend a great deal of time explaining to our young children not to put objects in their mouths, not to talk to strangers, and not to cross the street without looking. These are certainly important, as are things we attempt to have children master: eating with utensils, speaking clearly, and sharing their toys. By avoiding the topics of alcohol and other drugs, either by not bringing them up in class or by not answering simple questions, an opportunity to foster communication on these topics is missed.

Elementary school years provide an expanded world for our young. Children spend greater amounts of time away from home, are exposed to adult role models other than family members, develop peer groups, and experience personal growth. In many ways, their world is expanding and independence is sought. However, there is also a part of them that wishes not to be independent and still enjoys being a child. The importance of the family and school is maintained during this phase of life. Though the peer group is forming and re-forming throughout the later stage of elementary school, for most children it has not yet become as important as it will be.

The significance of alcohol and other drugs is often ignored during the elementary years. Most young people have been introduced to alcohol and are introduced to other drugs by observing others at home, school, on television, at the movies, or in advertisements. For many, the first drink occurs between the ages of ten and thirteen. This is usually at home, in the family setting and for appropriate reasons (as a beverage to celebrate a special event). However, this introduction is usually not discussed at home, nor is it often discussed at school. Generally, the educational system has supported society's opinion that young people don't have questions about alcohol and other drugs, and they can wait until they're older to begin discussing these topics.

Young people have many questions at this time that deserve to be acknowledged and answered. Some of these are: What is alcohol? Why do people drink? How does it make you feel? Why do people act differently after they've been drinking? Why do some people not drink? What are other drugs? Why do people use them? Are they all bad? How do they make you feel? Are they different from alcohol? How are they made? If we do not provide opportunities for these questions to be discussed, often the more advanced questions are not raised.

The upper elementary or junior high school years find our students in a period of transition. The importance of the peer group can be seen in what they wear, how they wear it, and when they wear it. Music of "in" groups fill their rooms where they spend a great deal of time. The telephone becomes a link to their world; they can converse on the phone while doing at least one other activity. One has to wonder sometimes if they are carrying on a conversation or just holding on for a sense of security and belonging. Scheduling meals and activities in a family becomes a major feat. This is a very lively and active time, during which we see dramatic physical changes. It can also be a difficult time for those who are developing too quickly or too slowly. No one seems to think they are developing appropriately. Youth often become extremely critical of their looks and are convinced that they're unattractive. They also believe that adults know nothing in some, if not most, areas. Great patience is necessary to deal effectively with this age, as is a strong sense of self-worth and a sense of humor.

Because adolescents spend a great deal of time challenging rules and regulations, we often overlook their great sensitivity, their unwillingness to appear not to know, and their desire to belong. Their alcohol and other drug questions might not have been answered by any of their sources; in fact, they might not even have been raised. Yet they do have important questions: What are the various alcoholic beverages? How are they made and are they different? What are the effects on the human body? What is the difference between being high, tight, tipsy, stoned, roasted? How much can I drink? How does being intoxicated feel? How much will make me intoxicated? Why are certain groups using other drugs? Where do they get them? How does it feel? What are the "goods" as well as the "bads" of other drugs? Why are certain drugs illegal? Why do most people seem to be looking the other way regarding drug availability? What happens to you if you try drugs? What will your parents do? What will the school do?

An equally important set of questions are personal and situational: What if someone spikes the punch at a party or passes around a joint? How should I act? What will I do? What will happen to me and my place in the group, or what will happen if my parents find out? If I want to refuse, what can I say? These and other questions need to be discussed, because even if the situation has not yet presented itself, the questions are still very real.

The high school years are often as trying as they are exciting. The independence/dependence conflict is still present in young people, and added stress is often produced by major life decisions that need to be made at this time. Students are experiencing, as well as experimenting, with a variety of activities: dating, driving, and part-time jobs. The peer group is still strong and very much a part of the high school scene. The person at this age will tell you he or she wears jeans and T-shirts because he or she wants to, not because everyone else might be wearing them. The fact that most are in this uniform is considered unimportant and irrelevant.

The desire for freedom in many areas of life is also an important aspect of this stage. Adolescents are very sensitive to being treated as children. It is often difficult to know *how* to treat them. Sometimes, when we say "act your age," we want them to be more compliant and act as we did when we were younger and other times we want them to act as adults.

They are learning many new things at this time and it tends to be overwhelming. School work, dating, driving, working after school, and partying may create more than a little juggling and perhaps some fear, apprehension, and anxiety. This should not cause us to dismiss this age and hope we all get through it quickly. It is a positive time in most respects, and one that has many unasked questions. Many of these questions are related to alcohol and other drug use or nonuse.

Other significant issues are:

Would anyone come to my party if I don't serve alcohol?

What could or would I do if someone brought alcohol or other drugs to the party?

How can I handle not drinking or taking drugs at a party?

How will the group react to my refusal?

How can I refuse if I feel like I've had enough?

How should I deal with intoxicated people?

What can I do if I'm in no condition to drive or if my friend is in no condition to drive?

How will the group feel if I don't go with an intoxicated driver?

What are the warning signs of an alcohol or other drug problem?

Should I try to help a friend with a problem, and how can I do it?

Obviously all questions and information needs are not resolved the day the young person completes high school. Many issues and situational questions continue through college, military service, and independent living. This later age is not touched upon lightly, and we do not want to imply that the questions are less important. We are just highlighting the years where our impact as educators is most significant. If we communicate with our students about alcohol and other drugs, we can be hopeful that the door will remain open for continued discussion.

Situations: Spontaneous and Planned

The door to discussion is often unintentionally closed throughout a student's life. This happens because we're unsure of or uncomfortable with a topic, we think it's controversial, or we just feel busy and overworked. It also happens on occasion because the push of the door is so gentle we're not aware of it. Children go through stages where everything they seem to be saying is in capital letters followed by exclamation marks. It's hard to sort through this and receive their clues. It is also easy to lose their brief and quiet statements when they're in another stage. Sometimes they want us to pursue a topic, and think that because they brought it up in passing we should realize its significance. We do miss some of these opportunities for spontaneous discussion. Others we let pass by and decide we'll discuss the topic later because the time is not right. In fact, they may have chosen that particular time knowing we were busy, so that if it was missed it had at least been stated.

Planned discussions are also important. However, we often shy away from planning an alcohol or other drug lesson because of our uneasiness about the topic or a desire not to confront the situation. It can also be caused by the fact that the community's position on alcohol and other drug education has not been clarified. We forget that by not discussing these issues our students decide they aren't appropriate topics, and they assume they know what's important. It is critical that feelings about alcohol and other drugs be discussed; that appropriate use be distinguished from high-risk, problematic use; and that acceptable alternatives be clarified.

Discussion may also center on our concern for someone who has an alcohol or other drug problem. Other discussions should focus on adolescent activities. If we accept the fact that alcohol and other drugs are available and might be present at a teenage party, the implications can be discussed. This is not meant to indicate that we must give our approval to any and all alcohol- or other drug-related behavior. It is meant to motivate communication on what is responsible and irresponsible. Hopefully, this discussion will also establish consequences for irresponsible behavior. In this way, young people won't have to assume what the consequences will be and won't be motivated to take risks.

We can aid our students in the decision making process by providing a safe and open forum for discussion. This gives students the opportunity of hearing the position and perspective of their peers. It also supports healthy decision making and the formulation of acceptable guidelines and alternatives.

In order to be comfortable with discussions on alcohol and other drugs, a framework needs to be established. This may be stated in school policy, a school system's statement of goals, or in a selected curriculum.

Student Outcomes for Chemical Health Curriculum

Though education about chemical use begins at home through communication with parents and parental models of behavior with alcohol and other drugs, it continues throughout a person's life by communication with friends, teachers, clergy, neighbors, and observation of others, including the media. The primary goal of school-based education programs is to help each student achieve a state of chemical health in which a young person makes personally and socially responsible decisions about use and nonuse of any chemical. This goal can be achieved by creating a learning environment that supports abstinence and responsibility to make healthy choices, and offers opportunities for students to acquire knowledge and develop skills that will enable them to make appropriate and safe choices.

The following chart is designed to assist teachers and curriculum developers identify essential student outcomes so that curriculum can be selected or developed reflecting anticipated goals and outcomes.

As a result of our efforts, students should know that:

SELF-AWARENESS

1. Each person is unique.
2. Each person experiences many emotions.
3. Each person communicates verbally and nonverbally.
4. How a person feels about him- or herself is an important factor in determining how one acts.
5. Feeling good is a common human need; children and adults seek a variety of ways to feel good.
6. All children and adults experience physical and emotional pain.
7. All people make mistakes.
8. All people experience predictable physical, emotional, and environmental changes (puberty, physical growth, intellectual growth) and unpredictable changes (accidents, death, illness, relocation, family separation).
9. All people have needs including, but not limited to, security, privacy, friendship, affection, a sense of freedom, and dignity.
10. Each person has personal strengths, skills, and interests.
11. A person's emotions impact on mood and behavior.
12. Changes in life circumstances occur.

SOCIAL SKILLS

13. People use a variety of decision making models.
14. All behavior has consequences.
15. All people experience some conflict in their relationships with others.
16. Communicating thoughts and feelings is a skill that can be developed.
17. Each person experiences stress throughout life.
18. Moral, social, and environmental factors influence personal decision making.
19. Each person has rights and responsibilities in a relationship with another person.
20. Communication is verbal and nonverbal.
21. Choices and their consequences are available.
22. Behaviors that are consistent with one's values can be identified and selected.
23. Risks which promote healthful behavior and minimize destructive behavior are acceptable.
24. Coping with difficult situations (teasing, conflict, job, physical pain, success, mistakes) can be learned.
25. Communicating feelings and thoughts openly, accurately and honestly, verbally and nonverbally, is healthy.
26. Listening to others' thoughts and feelings is important.
27. Deferred gratification can be accepted.
28. Assertiveness in relationships with others is positive.
29. Developing and maintaining friendships are necessary for social growth.
30. Conflicts with others can be resolved in a mutually satisfying way.

SOCIAL SYSTEMS

31. Children and adults live, work, and play in groups (social systems).
32. Each group has values, often unstated, which govern interaction among group members.

33. Support is available from family, friends, teachers, clergy, and community helpers.
34. Children and adults have choices to make about their lives.
35. Children and adults are responsible for their own behavior.
36. Behavior is influenced by other people and one's environment (socially, emotionally, physically).
37. Group membership is a choice.
38. Group membership choices are influenced by one's self-concept and the support of others.
39. Parent/child relationships change over time.
40. Groups significant to each person can be identified.
41. Individual differences among group members are probable and acceptable.
42. Functioning productively in a group is a key to positive interactions.
43. Influences for one's behavior can be identified.
44. Each person impacts on others.

CHEMICAL USE IN SOCIETY
45. A chemical is any substance used to produce physiological change within a person.
46. Chemicals are neither good nor bad. They can be used constructively or destructively.
47. Societal attitudes affect decisions about chemical use.
48. Each person makes decisions regarding personal use of alcohol and other drugs.
49. Chemical use may result in risks and consequences.
50. The person has a personal, as well as a group, responsibility toward helping his or her friends minimize risks.
51. People who are chemically dependent can recover and lead full and healthy lives.

Summary

The WHEN section focuses on the interests and needs of students related to alcohol and other drugs through various stages of growth and development. Spontaneous and planned discussion sections are explored from the perspective of both students and teachers. Establishment of philosophy and goals, necessary for the development of a comprehensive program is presented as are specific student outcomes in the areas of self-awareness, social skills, social systems, and chemical use in society.

The interrelatedness of these factors for program development and implementation is obvious. Yet it is often overlooked by anxious and concerned educators who want to begin an alcohol and other drug education program "yesterday." It is essential that the needs of the students and the goals of the program be determined if the program is to positively impact on behavior.

PART III: HOW

The HOW section focuses on the components necessary for incorporating an alcohol or other drug policy and program into a school's curriculum, communication techniques, and discussion exercises.

The following checklist briefly designates necessary items to be handled by people involved in the development of both the policy and the program. We want to stress that this checklist is not all-inclusive. However, it will provide a place to begin. We suggest that a school administrator designate a person responsible for carrying out each of the particular tasks as quickly as possible. Experience also taught us that determining a time line for completion kept the process moving and kept all the participants current with the tasks yet to be completed.

This checklist has been developed to assist each school district to review its current program for minimizing chemical use problems among students. It has been taken, in part, from *Chemical Health: School Athletics and Fine Arts Activities*,[15] published by Hazelden Foundation. The information gathered through the use of this checklist can then be used for making policy, procedure, and other program decisions.

Policy and Program Elements

I. A SUMMARY OF THE ADMINISTRATIVE CONCERNS AND QUESTIONS THAT EACH SCHOOL

BOARD OR GOVERNING BODY NEEDS TO ADDRESS
ARE AS FOLLOWS:

A. Identification of person(s) responsible for assessing, planning, implementing, and evaluating program efforts, recognizing the complexities of chemical use problems and the varying expertise of people.

  1. Has an ongoing advisory group or task force made up of administrators,* teachers,* parents,* students,* professional and support staff,* chemical dependency/ health professionals, maintenance and service personnel, and community leaders been organized? (While all of the people listed above are appropriate, those marked with an asterisk are essential.)

  2. Has building resource person(s) been identified to respond to crisis intervention situations?

  3. Has staff resource person(s) with professional training and appropriate experience been identified in each building to respond to student chemical use problems?

  4. Has someone been assigned responsibility for the coordination and development of alcohol and other drug abuse prevention curriculum K-12?

B. Systematic assessment of needs of school community for prevention, intervention, and aftercare support.

  1. Assessment of the needs of the school community:

    a. Have school policies and procedures been written or revised to reflect changes in state or federal laws?

    b. Have school policies and procedures for responding to student problems, i.e., chemical use, child abuse and neglect, and discipline been integrated where appropriate?

c. Have the different roles and responsibilities of school staff in the minimization of chemical use problems been clearly defined and communicated?

d. Have provisions been made to allow students to maintain academic progress while participating in a therapeutic treatment program?

e. Have procedures been developed for allowing students and staff to participate in support groups during the regular school schedule?

2. Assessment of resources available within the school:

a. Have all school staff been trained in chemical use problem prevention and intervention?

b. Have selected staff members received specialized training in chemical use problem prevention and intervention?

c. Are these special staff members being used effectively?

d. Are special services within the district, i.e., special education, social work, counseling, and health care currently available to students?

3. Assessment of the community resources available to the school:

a. Have cooperative relationships been established with existing public helping agencies — city, county, state, and federal?

b. Have cooperative relationships been established with local law enforcement agencies?

c. Is a listing of the private human service organizations available to the school district updated annually?

    d. Are the locations, dates, and phone numbers of Al-Anon, Alateen, and other support groups available to all students and staff?

C. Establishment of an ongoing evaluation and assessment process to promote appropriate programming and ensure flexibility of procedures:

    1. Is the district policy and procedures reviewed regularly?

    2. Is the alcohol and other drug education curriculum K-12 regularly reviewed and revised?

    3. Is an annual review of critical incidents, procedures, and referrals conducted?

II. TRAINING TO ENSURE THAT ALL STAFF HAVE THE KNOWLEDGE AND SKILLS TO IMPLEMENT EFFORTS TO MINIMIZE CHEMICAL USE PROBLEMS AMONG STUDENTS.

A. Are all staff aware of the school's responsibility to respond to student chemical use problems?

B. Have all school staff been made aware of chemical use and related problems, and specific purposes of prevention, intervention, therapy, and aftercare?

C. Have appropriate staff received information related to existing state laws, policies, and procedures for preventing and responding to student problems, i.e., chemical use, child abuse and neglect, and discipline?

D. Have prevention curriculum and instruction skills for appropriate staff been developed?

E. Has each staff member's responsibility and liability in responding to student problems, i.e., chemical use, child abuse and neglect, and discipline been clarified?

F. Have all staff had an opportunity to develop skills to

observe and report specific and identifiable behaviors of concern?

G. Are all staff aware of the needs of students returning to school after completing therapy/treatment or currently involved in outpatient therapy?

III. A SUMMARY OF PREVENTION AND HEALTH PROMOTING QUESTIONS THAT EACH SCHOOL BOARD OR OTHER GOVERNING BODY SHOULD CONSIDER IS AS FOLLOWS:

A. Have efforts been made to establish a caring school community with empathy, compassion, and communication extended between administrators, students, teachers, and parents?

B. Have efforts been made to establish an emotionally healthy classroom which includes emphasis on the development of a positive self-concept, coping skills, interpersonal relationships, decision making, and assertiveness?

C. Has a K-12 comprehensive health curriculum been established which includes emphasis on health promotion and chemical health issues?

D. Has pharmacological information been integrated into the K-12 curriculum appropriate to the student's age and environment? This should include specific information on the effects of chemical use in athletic and other activity performance.

E. Have prevention concepts and strategies been integrated into all curriculum areas?

F. Have the unique needs of students experiencing family problems, i.e., chemical use, child abuse and neglect, and family change been recognized?

G. Have support groups been established which provide

students and staff the opportunity to examine personal chemical use patterns?

H. Has the school district made efforts to establish programs to improve parent/student communication?

I. Has the district established and promoted programs in parenting skills for students and adults?

J. Does the district provide a healthy balance of extra-curricular and cocurricular activities which allows for students' self-development and creativity and recognizes individual needs, interests, and skill levels?

IV. A SUMMARY OF THE INTERVENTION QUES-TIONS EACH SCHOOL BOARD OR OTHER GOVERN-ING BODY SHOULD CONSIDER IS AS FOLLOWS:

A. Has the district developed procedures to follow when a staff member or student observes behavior which may indicate a chemical use problem or when a student seeks help?

B. Has the district developed procedures to follow when a staff member or student uses chemicals inappropriately or illegally while on school property or attending school functions? These procedures should follow due process and include provisions for 1) education regarding chemical use problems, 2) preassessment interview, and 3) disciplinary actions.

C. Has the district developed procedures for involving school personnel with a family or student troubled by chemical use problems?

D. Has the district developed a process to communicate with treatment or therapeutic programs regarding student needs and progress in accordance with existing state and federal confidentiality laws?

E. Has the district developed chemical use problem crisis intervention procedures to respond to medical emergencies, i.e., overdose or withdrawal situations?

F. Has the district developed procedures for transferring people to detoxification situations?

G. Has the district developed procedures to follow when a student is behaving in ways which may cause harm to self or others?

H. Has the district developed procedures to immediately notify a local county welfare department or law enforcement agency when abuse or neglect is suspected?

I. Has a group support system been established for people returning to the school community after completing therapy/treatment for chemical use problems?

J. Have cooperative relationships with community resources been established to help students returning to the school community after completing therapy/treatment?

K. Have provisions been made for special tutoring service when needed?

L. Have provisions been made to maintain communication with therapeutic/treatment programs regarding student needs and progress upon returning to school in accordance with existing state and federal confidentiality laws?

Communication Techniques

Whether communication is spontaneous or planned, there are some basic techniques that will help. The first is to relax. If we are tense and uptight, the atmosphere will be strained and uncomfortable for everyone. Alcohol and other drug issues are sensitive topics. Students often expect us to be on the opposite side and not understand their position. Therefore, our tone is a critical factor in the communication process. An open, honest, and nonthreatening atmosphere will facilitate discussion. Sharing with and by our students cannot result in punishment if we hope to continue communicating. It also must encourage participation by all and shouldn't turn into a lecture. And, everyone's opinion must be valued and respected. This must also include the educators' opinions. As adults with knowledge and experience, we can provide information about risks, consequences, and benefits of chemical use that students may not consider. Respecting students' ideas does not preclude sharing our own thoughts and feelings.

It is also important that we are comfortable with the topic. Think about your own use of alcohol and other drugs, activities in your home related to alcohol and other drug use, and information you've read. Accept the fact that there might be things you haven't thought about and questions to which you don't have answers. It's okay to say, "I'll have to think about that," or, "I don't know." This is being honest, another significant ingredient in communication. If we expect students to open up and share with us, then we must do the same. Honest feelings and information will generate healthy discussion and set the stage for the process to continue.

Understand that this process is designed for participation. Without student involvement in the process, communication ceases. Their statements and questions should be accepted in a manner that reinforces their good feelings about the communication process. A negative attitude toward their contributions will be viewed as a put-down and will be a signal to withdraw. This does not mean questions cannot be asked by us or by them; however, they should be clarifying or informational questions.

Some discussion exercises are provided to help you begin the process, to stimulate discussion, and to provide additional items to maintain the process.

Discussion Exercises

A variety of discussion exercises is presented. These are questions, role plays, and vignettes; feel free to skip exercises you're not ready to try, but try not to bypass a topic area because you don't think it's necessary. Your students may want to discuss alcohol and other drug use, drug problems, and/or how to handle refusing chemicals. Since young people don't have many opportunities for practicing refusal skills, this type of discussion should be very helpful.

Discussion Questions

Discussion questions often help introduce a topic and motivate communication. The following alcohol and other drug questions are designed to stimulate discussion:

ALCOHOL:
How do you feel about drinking?

Why do some people drink? Why do you think some people decide not to drink?

What characterizes responsible and appropriate alcohol use?

How do you feel about teenage drinking? What has made you feel this way?

Is alcohol a part of the adolescent social scene in your community?

Are there pressures to drink to be part of this scene?

How can people respond to pressure to drink? What would make a student comfortable in this role?

If alcohol is served at parties, how will the situation be handled? Who will monitor the situation?

How will intoxication be minimized? What can and should be done if someone gets intoxicated?

If no alcohol is to be served, how can you deal with someone who brings alcohol to the party?

What are acceptable alternatives for getting home if the driver
  has been drinking?
Would there be consequences if the alternatives were chosen?
  If so, what would these be? How would the intoxicated
  driver respond?

OTHER DRUGS:
How do you feel about using drugs?
Why do some people use drugs? Why do you think some
  people decide not to use drugs?
What characterizes responsible and appropriate drug use?
  Legal? Illegal?
Are there risks related to using drugs? If so, what are they?
Are drugs a part of the adolescent social scene in your com-
  munity?
Are there pressures to use drugs to be part of this scene?
How can people respond to pressure to use drugs? What
  would make a student comfortable in this role?
If drugs are a part of parties, how will the situation be
  handled? Who will monitor the situation?
How can problems be minimized? What can and should be
  done if someone gets stoned?
If drugs are not to be used, how can you deal with someone
  who brings drugs to the party?
What are acceptable alternatives for getting home if the driver
  is impaired?
Would there be consequences if the alternatives were chosen?
  If so, what would these be? How would the impaired driver
  respond?

Role Playing

Role playing is fun and can also motivate meaningful
discussion. It is a relatively simple technique where an activity
or situation is described. Those participating try to think how
they would feel and respond in the described situation.

Observers should be thinking about how they would react in the same scene and what changes would alter the outcome.

A party guest trying to refuse a drink from a pushy host/ hostess.

An adolescent trying to convince his or her parent to not stay home during a party.

A parent trying to convince a teenager that parents should stay home during a party.

A friend refusing to get in the car with an intoxicated driver.

A teenager's response to the offer of marijuana.

A friend trying to convince another that he or she is too intoxicated to drive.

A parent dealing with an intoxicated adolescent.

A friend explaining to another that he or she thinks the person has an alcohol or other drug problem.

A parent trying to motivate an adolescent to have a party, even though alcohol and other drugs will not be allowed.

Vignettes

The use of short stories to stimulate discussion is a technique that has been modified in the following stories. Endings are not provided so each person can decide how the story will conclude. This is done to allow teachers and students to share their reasons and perspective for each situation.

After a party, three young men gather on the front lawn of a friend's house. It is 2:00 A.M. and time for them to be heading home. Chuck, the driver of the car, has obviously had too much to drink, and Joe is also feeling good and in no hurry to go anywhere. Mark is not high and is very uneasy about riding home with Chuck. Chuck opens the car door and . . .

Four female teenagers are talking in a secluded section of an almost empty playground. Mary Jo has a bottle of vodka in a brown paper bag. As it gets dark, she opens the bottle, takes a drink, and encourages the others to have some and pass it around. Suzie is delighted and can't wait for her turn; Julie senses the excitement in the air and, though she's a little unsure, has decided to take her share. Margie is inwardly very upset. She is a nondrinker and knows her family doesn't approve of alcohol. She does not want to drink and is trying to decide how to handle the situation. When the bottle is passed to her, she . . .

It seems to Lynn as if everyone at school has tried marijuana but Lynn. She has avoided certain people and places because she's been afraid she'll be in an awkward situation. Sleeping over at her friend Jo's house has always been fun until tonight. Jo got a joint from her sister and she wants Lynn to share it. As Jo closes the bedroom door, Lynn . . .

Tim and Jane are on their first date and go to a party given by a teenager whose folks are away. Beer is plentiful, and the punch has been spiked. Tim has always enjoyed a few drinks at home or at a party. He is comfortable if his drinks are paced, and he doesn't like to feel pushed to drink more than he wants. Jane doesn't drink very often, but when she does she tends to get intoxicated. As she is obviously getting high, Tim realizes he is becoming extremely uncomfortable. Tim asks Jane to take a walk outside and . . .

Mr. Jones, a corporate executive, is Bob's boss. Since this is Bob's first job after graduation, he is trying very hard to do well and please Mr. Jones. Yet no matter how hard he tries, he can't seem to satisfy his boss. Mr. Jones is argumentative and nasty, especially after lunch. On days when Mr. Jones doesn't return from lunch, Bob covers for him and makes excuses as to why he's not in the office. Occasionally, Mr. Jones seems pleased, but if Bob mentions he couldn't reach him, Mr. Jones flies into a rage. Though

Bob often smells alcohol on Mr. Jones' breath, he's not sure alcohol is the problem. However, he is sure Mr. Jones has a problem; Bob also knows he is having more trouble than usual. Mr. Jones threatened to fire Bob this morning. Bob has to do something and decides to . . .

The salespeople of a large company are under a great deal of pressure to increase sales. Since most sales meetings with clients begin with lunch, John, Mark, and Lorraine are busily attempting to make appointments with clients. Mark and Lorraine have discussed what five lunches in a restaurant can do to their diet. They've also discussed how alcohol affects their abilities and have worked out some techniques to refuse a drink or to have only one. John ignores these conversations because he enjoys drinking at lunch and, in fact, seems to only want to call clients that enjoy it as well. Lorraine and Mark don't understand why John invites only some of his clients to lunch and are resentful of the fact that he isn't using all his contacts. When they ask, "What about so and so," he says he'll get to them later. Mark and Lorraine . . .

Claire's office buddies have invited her to a party at Bud's house on Friday night. Getting together with her friends is always fun, and Claire is delighted to be at the party, especially after having such a bad week. She's had a couple of drinks and a plate of food and is really enjoying herself. As a few of the people start to leave, Claire is debating whether she should go home. Though she usually leaves early, she decides to treat herself and stay to the end. As everyone settles down, the atmosphere becomes more mellow. As Claire congratulates herself on deciding to stay, Herbert announces that he's brought a few joints and now that the "squares" have left, they can really enjoy them-selves. Claire is excited about the prospect and, at the same time, feels somewhat trapped. She . . .

Anne is always busy and involved with at least four projects at one time. Lately everything takes more time than Anne has, and she's burning the candle at both ends. Todd is as busy as Anne but seems to have plenty of energy. When Anne says she just won't make it if she doesn't get some sleep, Todd offers to share his secret — uppers . . .

A Note for Teachers

Additional techniques for communicating with your students about alcohol and other drugs can be designed by you with help from your students. It is also possible that you have only needed a few of the discussion exercises and were able to follow through in a less structured manner. In either case, the goal of sharing information, feelings, and attitudes is the same. It is not necessary that we all use the same strategies or even all agree on what issues are important. The fact that we're motivating open and honest communication provides the atmosphere where topics and problems can be discussed.

Summary

How to talk to students about alcohol and other drugs is discussed through policy and program elements, communication techniques, and discussion exercises. The teacher's comfort with the topic will facilitate and motivate discussion. Students can then discuss situations and behaviors on which they desire more information and a perspective from their peers. In this manner, the peer group can develop into a positive support system for healthy and responsible decisions.

PART IV: WHAT IF

Problems related to the use of alcohol and other drugs might include bringing alcohol into the school dance and winding up in trouble with school authorities, coming home intoxicated and getting into trouble with parents, or smoking marijuana in the park and getting caught by the police. These incidents are troublesome and may put a young person in a serious risk situation. Drinking and driving is another example of a person in a high-risk situation. An adolescent may not have been able to judge the state of intoxication and decided to drive.

Though this may cause serious harm to the person and others, it may not be chemical dependency; however, it warrants serious concern. A rare incident or a problem related to alcohol or other drugs necessitates communication and concern. A series of incidents and frequent problems related to alcohol or other drugs may require treatment. How to know when to talk and when to act is difficult to put into perspective. Some identifying behaviors of concern will be discussed.

Identifying Behaviors of Concern

Teachers, school nurses, guidance counselors, coaches, activity directors, and other concerned staff are in a unique position to observe students in a variety of settings. Every

STUDENT ASSISTANCE PROCESS
FLOWCHART III[16]

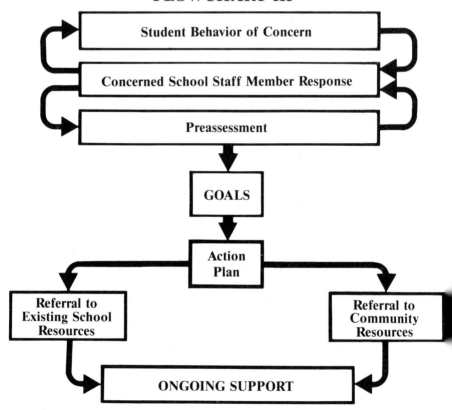

Student Behavior of Concern

Concerned School Staff Member Response

Preassessment

GOALS

Action Plan

Referral to Existing School Resources

Referral to Community Resources

ONGOING SUPPORT

school staff member has the potential to indentify behavior and determine if it is inappropriate, unacceptable, and irresponsible. It is important to remember simple identification of problem behavior is all that is asked of the school staff member; in fact, it is all that is wanted. It is important that some kind of record be kept of the behavior including where and when it was observed. Some behaviors associated with a chemical use problem are listed below. While anyone can identify these behaviors, only those professionally trained should make a diagnosis or evaluation of conditions such as alcoholism or chemical dependency.

a. Absenteeism from school, class, or practice.
b. Tardiness to class or practice.
c. Diminishing quality of assignments or performance.
d. Trouble with peers.
e. Hostility toward staff members.
f. Changes in appearance.
g. Changes in after-school activities.
h. Obvious chemical use.
i. Involvement in arguments, fights, thefts, or other illegal behavior.
j. Noticeable change in friends over a period of time.
k. Attitude changes.
l. Any other changes that compel attention.

It should be pointed out that many of these behaviors are not necessarily related to inappropriate chemical use. They could be associated with emotional, family, physical, eating, social, legal, or sexual problems. Nevertheless, if the behaviors or concern persists for any length of time, the concerned staff member should tell the student about these observed behavior changes, share personal concern, and offer help. It is important that school staff members document or record specific behaviors of concern. The date, time, location, and description of the behavior should be noted. This will eliminate any confusion over what took place and address a common student perception that "you are picking on me."

It is clearly the right and responsibility of caring, concerned school staff to discuss such behavior with those for whom we have responsibility. The difficulty often arises in not knowing what to say. Perhaps the key to unlocking this is simple, honest feedback. Directly telling the student what behavior has been observed and expressing how you felt when you observed that behavior is the most appropriate response. Many problems can and will be resolved simply because of concern and feedback shown by others. In some cases, the problems observed may not be resolved by communication with a caring, concerned person. You may discover a complex and serious problem you are not prepared to handle, or you may be confronted by an angry, upset, or uncooperative student who chooses not to respond. If this happens, it is important to refer the student to a student assistance person or another school support staff such as a counselor, social worker, or nurse.

Student Assistance Program

The student assistance person or team is designated to follow up referrals from concerned people. To be more specific, the student assistance person should:
  a. Respond to referrals received from teachers and other staff.
  b. Assess the nature and extent of problems.
  c. Make appropriate referrals to existing school programs or to community resources such as social service agencies, treatment settings, etc.
  d. Provide follow up by monitoring the student's progress in the referred program.
  e. Communicate to teachers, parents, and administrators the progress of the student, while respecting federal and state confidentiality and right-to-privacy laws.
  f. Monitor the program's effectiveness with individual cases.

PART V: CONCLUSION

Effective alcohol and other drug education must consider the pluralistic nature of our society and the diverse use patterns and attitudes present in the community. Youthful alcohol and other drug use and relevant issues for this population should also be integrated into the philosophy and goals of the program. Teacher training, content needs of students, and school policies are necessary supporting elements to assure the program's success.

Education has the potential to significantly impact our nation's youth by providing realistic information and helping students develop skills to prevent problems. It also has the power to assist young people having problems related to their alcohol or other drug use or such use by a family member. Viable and relevant alcohol education belongs in the elementary school, the junior high school, the high school, and the college or university system.

To assure its effectiveness, professionals need to be trained and the institution has to support the program by its attitude, policies, and practices toward alcohol and other drugs. Ambivalence and misinformation will not be eliminated without positive action from the educational community.

APPENDIX A:
ALCOHOL AND OTHER
DRUGS

Alcohol

Alcohol was probably discovered quite by accident when early man left fruits, berries, or vegetables out in the air. When the juice of these items was consumed, the discovery of beverage alcohol occurred. Obviously, primitive man found the taste and effects pleasurable and decided to continue duplicating the event. It was, and is, relatively easy to produce alcoholic beverages because the process of fermentation occurs naturally. Fermentation begins when the juice of fruits, berries, or vegetables is left unsealed in the air. The sugar in the juice reacts with yeast, a microscopic plant which floats freely in the air. This reaction continues until the juice contains approximately 12% to 14% alcohol. Since this amount of alcohol is enough to stop the action of the yeast, the process finishes and the juice is now wine. Beer is also produced by the process of fermentation.

Other alcoholic beverages are made by the process of distillation. When a fermented beverage (wine or beer) is heated in a still, the alcohol separates from the mixture as a vapor. Since water and other ingredients remain in the liquid state, the alcohol vapor can be captured and cooled. As the vapor cools, it returns to a liquid state and is almost pure alcohol. Flavoring and water are then added to produce the desired beverage. This process is used to make whiskey (rye, scotch, bourbon) vodka, and rum.

It is possible for a manufacturer to produce a distilled beverage with any amount of alcohol. However, the manufacturer is required by law to list the degrees of proof on the label. If you divide the proof by two, you can determine the percentage of alcohol in the beverage. That is, 86-proof whiskey contains 43% alcohol. Since it is the alcohol in the beverage that produces the effects on the body, the percentage of alcohol is important. This brings us to another significant point. Many people think the percentage of alcohol by volume in various beverages makes one or two of them less intoxicating; beer contains 3 to 6% alcohol; wine contains 12 to 14%; and distilled spirits contain 40 to 50%. If the beverages are compared in the same volume, (1-1/2 oz. of beer, 1-1/2 oz. of wine, and 1-1/2 oz. of distilled spirits), the beer does contain less alcohol than the wine, and the wine has less alcohol than distilled spirits. However, beer and wine drinkers don't usually measure their drinks by, or drink from, a shot glass. When we compare the amount of alcohol in beer, wine, and distilled spirits in their normal servings, we find there is approximately the same amount of alcohol in 12 oz. of beer, 5 oz. of wine, and 1-1/2 oz. of distilled spirits.

The effects of alcohol on the body are produced by the amount of alcohol consumed, not the type of beverage. The effects also depend on a number of other significant factors.

Body weight: This factor is often overlooked because many people don't realize alcohol is dispersed through the blood and the body's fluids. Therefore, the higher the body weight, the greater the volume of blood through which the alcohol is dispersed and the lower the concentration of alcohol in the blood.

Size of drink and quantity of alcohol consumed: The size of the drink and the quantity of alcohol consumed are related factors. The normal quantity or size of a drink is 12 oz. of beer, 5 oz. of wine, and 1-1/2 oz. of distilled spirits. If the drink consumed is smaller or larger, the effects on the body will be different. This is important to understand; if a person has a double, the amount of alcohol will be doubled. Quantity of alcohol consumed directly influences the effects on the body. The more alcohol consumed, the greater the effects will be.

Length of time: Time is a critical, but often overlooked, factor. The body is only able to eliminate a certain amount of alcohol per hour. If the person spaces his or her drinks, then the effects of alcohol will not be as severe when compared with the same amount of alcohol consumed in a short period of time.

Food in the stomach: Since the effects of alcohol on the body are not felt by the person until the alcohol is in the bloodstream, food is helpful because it slows the process of alcohol absorption.

In addition, alcohol's effects on the person also depend on the feelings and expectations of the drinker and the person's experience in drinking. That is, alcohol will increase or heighten a person's positive or negative feelings and often supply the results the drinker anticipated.

The effects of alcohol on the body depend on the variety of factors discussed as well as the quantity of alcohol consumed. The quantity, blood alcohol concentration (BAC), and effects on the body are as follows:

	BAC	Effects
1 drink	.03%	relaxation; slight feeling of exhilaration.
2 drinks	.06%	slowed response/reaction time; poor muscle control; slurred speech.
3 drinks	.09%	clouded judgment; lessened self-restraint; impaired decision-making ability.
4 drinks	.12%	blurred vision; unclear speech; lack of coordination of hands; unsteadiness.

The person described in the chart weighs 160 pounds. The effects would be less per drink for a person who weighed more than 160 pounds; the effects would occur with fewer drinks if the person weighed less than that. It is also necessary to consider the factor of time. The chart implies that the drinks were consumed at one point in time. If the four drinks were consumed over a longer period of time, the BAC would be lower and the effects at a comparably lower level.

The body constantly works to eliminate alcohol that has been consumed. This occurs in two ways: elimination and oxidation. Elimination rids the body of only about 10% of ingested alcohol by way of the lungs (the alcohol evaporates in the air) and the kidneys (a small amount of alcohol is removed from the blood by the kidneys and passes out of the body as urine). The remaining 90% or so is removed from the body by oxidation (uniting of a substance with oxygen), which takes place in the liver. However, the liver can only oxidize a small amount of alcohol at one time; the remaining alcohol continues to circulate in the body and returns to the liver for oxidation. This process continues until all alcohol is eliminated. The oxidation rate for a person weighing 160 pounds is approximately seven grams of alcohol per hour. That is, it takes about two hours for the body to eliminate the alcohol consumed in one drink, four hours for two drinks, eight hours for four drinks, etc.

It should be noted that most people consume alcohol as a beverage to relax, to be social, to enjoy a party, and to stimulate appetite. This consumption may take place at home, at a party, as part of a religious ceremony, or in a restaurant. Drinking is most frequently done with others and is usually secondary to the event or activity. This doesn't imply that the drinking described does not occasionally result in high-risk situations or in problems related to the use of alcohol. However, the majority of people who consume alcohol are not problem drinkers or alcoholics. (Alcoholism is discussed in Appendix B).

Other Drugs

Discussing drugs other than alcohol is more difficult. There are many drugs, and their effects on the body are as varied as the number of substances classified as drugs. An interesting aside and a way of introduction to other drugs is: How shall information on drugs be presented? Should we discuss good and bad drugs? The good ones being prescribed medicines and over-the-counter remedies, the bad ones being "street drugs." This doesn't work when one thinks of a prescribed medicine (e.g., Valium) that might be obtained for sale on the street. Is it then a bad drug because of the manner of sale, or because there is not a physician monitoring its use?

We could also consider discussing drugs manufactured legally and those manufactured illegally. This consideration is difficult because some legally prescribed drugs are illegally produced and sold. It is also difficult because illegal drugs are not always what their label says; also, there is no quality control in their manufacture and the dose might not correspond to the dose in a legally manufactured drug.

We could also discuss drugs by the age of the consumer and have adult drugs and youth drugs. Though discussing patterns and habits of drug use in the youthful population is helpful, it won't aid us in our understanding of drugs. The other plan considered for discussing drugs is related to use. That would provide us with a category of medically used drugs (prescribed), recreational drugs (nonprescribed and taken for effects), and a multitude of categories in between.

It is also possible to consider drugs in the categories listed in the Controlled Substance Act or to present drugs in relationship to their potential for abuse. Drugs could also be categorized as those derived directly from nature or those produced synthetically. The variety of ways of discussing drugs tells us a great deal about our thinking or, more accurately perhaps, our *not* thinking about drugs.

Our information about drugs will be represented using the following categories: over-the-counter, prescribed, stimulants, depressants, narcotics, marijuana, and hallucinogens. This format was chosen because it meets the needs teachers require and also because the general categories are somewhat familiar. Hopefully, it will also enable us to consider the potential for abuse of substances not always considered as drugs or thought of in terms of drug-taking behaviors. Over-the-counter drugs and their effects will be presented first.

Over-the-counter drugs are those we purchase in drugstores and supermarkets. We store them in medicine cabinets and use them as home remedies for minor discomforts and annoyances (headaches, indigestion, and colds). When directions are followed, most over-the-counter medicines are safe and effective for most people. However, it must be pointed out that if other substances (e.g., other over-the-counter drugs, alcohol, prescribed drugs) are also taken at the same time as over-the-counter medications, a harmful drug interaction may occur. Though this stands to reason, our society is not generally aware of this. We probably owe our casual attitude toward over-the-counter substances to our growing up not thinking of them as drugs.

Over-the-counter products include such items as analgesics (aspirin and Tylenol compounds) used to reduce fever and eliminate various aches and pains; antacids (Alka-Seltzer, Maalox, Mylanta) used to neutralize hydrochloric acid in the stomach; sedatives (Nite Rest, Sure-Sleep, Sominex) used to induce sleep; antihistamines (Benadryl, Chlor-Trimeton, Ornade) used to alleviate allergy symptoms; cold remedies (Contac, Dristan) used to relieve cold symptoms; laxatives (Ex-Lax, Feen-a-Mint, Laxaid) used to eliminate constipation; and relaxants (Compoz, Seedate) used to calm us down and enable us to cope.

Other over-the-counter substances are mouthwashes, vitamins and minerals, antiperspirants, dental products, contraceptive products, hemorrhoidals, sunburn treatments, hair preparations, skin treatments, eye medications, and various other internal and external products. When one counts the various brand items of the same product and considers the variety of substances, the number of over-the-counter products is hard to believe. There are approximately one-half million over-the-counter products available for our use. We must be aware that it is possible to become dependent on these products, that it is possible to produce a serious side effect by overusing these products or by combining their use with other drugs. Our attitude toward these products is very much a part of our feelings and use of drugs.

Prescribed drugs also need to be discussed. As a society we are very comfortable with prescription drugs. This is due to our belief in the medical profession and our knowledge that drugs are made correctly and given to us for our well-being. However, it should be noted that there are over one hundred thousand prescription drugs available. Unwanted side effects may occur, and serious drug interactions may also occur when another drug is in the body. It is also possible to become dependent on prescription medication. People have been known to use more than one doctor and also more than one pharmacy to have an available supply of a particular drug. Though it is difficult for us to think of these people as chemically dependent, they are.

Some of the most commonly prescribed drugs in our country are tranquilizers (Valium, Librium), antibiotics (Ampicillin, V-Cillin K, Tetracycline HCI), narcotic analgesics (Tylenol with Codeine, Darvon Compound 65, Empirin Compound Codeine), diuretics (Anhydron, Diuril, Enduron), and oral contraceptives (Enovid, Norinyl, Oracon). There is a multitude of prescription drugs in addition to those noted.

It is estimated that every physician in the United States writes between five and ten thousand prescriptions a year.

Taking prescribed medicine must also be considered in terms of our drug using behaviors. Even though prescriptions are written and monitored by a physician and filled by a pharmacist, the person must be aware that he or she is taking a drug. It is also necessary to follow the instructions for these drugs. Not reading labels on over-the-counter drugs can be dangerous; not reading labels on prescription drugs can be catastrophic. We must become informed consumers regarding prescription drugs, as well as over-the-counter medications. It is also necessary for us to continually remind ourselves that prescription medications are part of drug taking in our society.

Stimulants are substances whose reaction results in an excitation of the central nervous system; that is, they make us feel "up." Unthinkingly, we consume a variety of stimulants on a regular basis. Caffeine (the active ingredient in coffee, tea, and cola drinks) is a stimulant used as a pick-me-up by many. Nicotine (in the form of tobacco) is also a frequently used stimulant. These are common in our society and not often thought of as drugs or considered in the issue of drug taking. Other stimulants, such as amphetamines, are thought of as drugs. This may be due to the potency of these substances and/or their reasons for use.

Amphetamines (dextroamphetamine, methamphetamine) are powerful stimulants. These are synthetic substances used since the 1930s. Up until the mid-1960s, the use of amphetamines was restricted to prescriptions for depression, increase of endurance, and weight loss. The mid-1960s found amphetamines on the "street," supplied by the black market. Increased use and misuse, as well as curtailment of legal production, have resulted in the emergence of illegal laboratory production of amphetamines and in higher cost of the drug. Illegal amphetamines are easily obtained in the black market and are often used by students, night-shift workers, professional drivers, housewives, athletes, and others. Some use is limited to the need for staying awake, greater amounts of endurance, and dieting; other use is specifically to experience euphoric pleasures. These uses result in the same dangers associated with amphetamine abuse: psychological dependence, sweating, inability to sleep, loss of appetite, fear, dry mouth, irregular heart beat, or irresponsible behavior. Large doses of amphetamines can result in death. If amphetamines are used on a regular basis, exhaustion may be masked and the person placed in a high-risk situation (driving an automobile or truck in a state of physical exhaustion). If the amphetamine use is stopped, the person may suffer sleepiness, nightmares, severe mental irritability, and great hunger.

Cocaine is also a powerful stimulant and an anesthetic. It is legally classified as a narcotic, though chemically it is not in this category. Cocaine is derived from the coca leaf. In the late 1880s, cocaine and caffeine were ingredients in the syrup called Coca-Cola. Cocaine was also an ingredient in many over-the-counter medications at that time. By 1903, cocaine was removed from Coca-Cola and shortly thereafter also removed from many medications. Cocaine was associated with undesirables (prostitutes and criminals), and its sale was prohibited except by prescription in 1914. However, cocaine found its way to the street and has been available illegally since that time. Its use seems to be on the upswing today as it produces euphoria, a feeling of energy and stimulation, and an increase of activity. Though cocaine is expensive, its use is turning up in various segments of the population. It is called snow, coke, flake, and other names on the street. Though tolerance does not occur, a psychological dependence on the feelings produced can develop. Extremely high doses of cocaine may interfere with respiration and the action of the heart. It is also possible to take a lethal dose of cocaine.

Depressants are often called "downers" as they depress the central nervous system, decreasing the person's awareness of the environment and activity. The most commonly used and misused depressant is alcohol. Other depressants are sedative-hypnotic drugs including barbiturates, tranquilizers, and anesthetics. Though narcotics are often classified as depressants, they will be discussed separately.

Barbiturates in small doses relieve tension and anxiety; larger doses produce effects similar to drunkenness (slurred speech, lack of coordination, slowed reaction time). Though they are legally available only by prescription, they are also illegally available on the street. The dangers of barbiturate use are: high-risk situations such as driving when one is impaired by the drug, the threat of life when combined with alcohol or other depressants, and the potential for physical dependence. If a person is dependent on barbiturates or other sedative- hypnotics, abrupt withdrawal of the drug may cause the person to suffer serious withdrawal symptoms (convulsions).

Major tranquilizers, derived from phenothiazine (Thorazine, Mellaril, and Compazine), are primarily prescribed for treating mental illness as they induce calmness, decrease temperature and blood pressure, and do not result in nausea or convulsions. These drugs do not produce physical or psychological dependence; however, if they are used in conjunction with other depressants, they may result in death. It is rare that these drugs are found in the illegal marketplace. However, this is not the case with minor tranquilizers (derived from benzodiazepine), as these are readily available on the street.

Minor tranquilizers are very popular drugs in our society; they are prescribed to reduce anxiety and tension. Some common examples of minor tranquilizers are Miltown, Equanil, Librium, and Valium. Physical dependence and severe withdrawal symptoms are associated with these drugs.

Anesthetics are potent nervous system depressants which render a part of the body insensitive to pain as a local anesthetic and induce sleep or produce unconsciousness as a general anesthetic. As a person goes through the stages of general anesthesia, he or she experiences a period of excitement prior to losing consciousness. Ether and chloroform are general anesthetics, as is Phencyclidine (PCP). PCP was developed as an animal tranquilizer and is the most widely abused of the anesthetics. When PCP is taken by humans, they hallucinate, become aggressive, and have difficulty with motor coordination and speech. Heavy doses may result in coma or death. Significant concern raised over the use of PCP is further complicated by the fact that on occasion it has been sprayed on marijuana.

Narcotics are depressants derived from opium plants or produced synthetically. They are chemically similar to opiates. Narcotics laws list the opiates (opium, morphine, and codeine), the derived or synthetic substitutes (heroin, dilaudid), and cocaine. Since cocaine was discussed in the section on stimulants, our discussion of narcotics will include only the opiates, opiate derivatives, and synthetic substances similar in effect.

Narcotics depress the central nervous system, produce sedation, relieve pain, reduce hunger and thirst, induce lethargy, and minimize the sex drive. In large doses they may result in coma and death. Physical addiction and psychological dependence may result from continued use because these drugs alter the body's normal functioning. If the drug is withdrawn abruptly, the body may find it impossible to function. Narcotics are prescribed for pain, and their use is carefully monitored. However, they are also part of the street drug scene, and it is estimated that over one-half million Americans are addicted to legal and illegal narcotics.

Marijuana is classified as a narcotic in the legal system, as an hallucinogen by some, and as a sedative-hypnotic by others. It is obtained from the plant *cannabis sativa* and contains the active chemical ingredient THC (tetrahydrocannabinol). Though marijuana has been used in various civilizations for hundreds of years, its most recent notoriety began with its widely publicized use in the 1960s. Cannabis is usually smoked as marijuana in cigarettes or bongs (pipes) and as hashish (the pure resin and most potent form) in an assortment of pipes. Since marijuana is not one uniform substance but may be a mixture of various parts of the plant, it is difficult to discuss its long-term impact on individual health. In fact, the debate about marijuana being a mild drug or a dangerous one has raged for the past fifteen years. Though the debate continues, some facts are known and generally accepted. The effects of marijuana are directly related to its strength and amount smoked. The high that is experienced provides a sense of euphoria and relaxation; it also alters time and space perception. With higher doses, the immediate memory may be impaired, thought may be fragmented, and a person's sense of identity may be altered. At very high doses, the person may experience visual distortions, an unreal sense of the body, and paranoid thinking. The setting and surroundings where marijuana is smoked may also be significant in determining marijuana's effect.

Though marijuana is not physically addicting, a tolerance may develop causing the person to increase the dose to experience the desired effects. It is also possible to develop a psychological dependence. Other investigations on marijuana use are continuing: What are the long-term effects of use on the person? Does marijuana cause chromosome damage resulting in birth defects? Does marijuana damage secondary sex characteristics? What is the effect of prolonged use on memory? What heart and lung problems may be attributed to marijuana use? Though questions abound, the answers will not be found simply or quickly. Unfortunately, while the questions remain unanswered, the marijuana-using population is growing. It also must be pointed out that, though the answers regarding long-term impact on the person are not available, regular use by the young population may impair their ability to function in educational and social growth experiences.

Hallucinogens produce changes in consciousness and are able to disorganize nerve and ego functions. While under the influence of an hallucinogen, the person may experience pleasant and exciting sensations or horrifying and terrifying sensations (i.e., "bad trip").

LSD (d-lysergic acid diethylamide tartrate 25) is one of the best known and most potent hallucinogens. The effects of LSD may include nausea, physiological changes (loss of appetite), and behavior changes. Dramatic mood swings, time and space distortion, and hallucinations may also be part of the trip. In addition, a recurrence of the trip may appear up to eighteen months following the taking of LSD.

STP (DOM) is another hallucinogen known for bad trips. It, too, distorts time, alters body sensations, and produces rapid mood swings. Though it is less potent than LSD, it is more potent than mescaline.

Mescaline is the chief active chemical in peyote. In sufficient doses, mescaline results in nausea, disorganized behavior and hallucinations; in high doses, heart and respiration rates are slowed.

Psilocybin, DMT (N-, N-dimethyltryptomine, *DET* (diethyltry ptamine), and *MDA* (2,3- Methylenediozyamphetamine) are also hallucinogens.

Though you may be overwhelmed by the number and variety of available drugs, it is important that you be some-what familiar with the major drugs and their effects. Did it surprise you that some "good" drugs become "bad" drugs due to how and where they are obtained and for the reasons and patterns of use? Hopefully, this has given you cause to ponder society's attitudes toward drugs and drug taking. More important, did the information motivate you to think about:

How and when you use drugs?
Why you use drugs?
What is appropriate drug use?
What is inappropriate drug use?
How you feel about drugs and their use?

This appendix on alcohol and other drugs is provided to offer information, stimulate your thinking, and clarify your attitudes. It is not meant to make you drug experts but rather to acquaint you with the various main categories of drugs available in society. If it has whetted your appetite for additional, detailed information, excellent reference sources are provided in the bibliography.

APPENDIX B: CHEMICAL DEPENDENCY

Alcohol and other drug problems are presented separately to provide perspective and information on each area. However, when drug dependent people are discussed, the drug of their choice is one factor; other elements of chemical dependency may be similar. The Expert Committee on Addiction-Producing Drugs of the World Health Organization has defined addiction as:

a state of periodic or chronic intoxication produced by the repeated consumption of a drug (natural or synthetic), which produces the following characteristics: (1) an overpowering desire or compulsion to continue taking the drug and to obtain it by any means; (2) a tendency to increase the dosage, showing body tolerance; (3) a psychic and, generally, a physical dependence on the effects of the drug; and (4) the creation of an individual and social problem.[17]

Alcoholism

Alcoholism is "a chronic disease manifested by repeated implicative drinking so as to cause injury to the drinker's health or to his social or economic functioning."[18] The disease develops over a period of time and is represented by a loss of control over the use of alcohol and a problem caused by drinking in a major life area: home, work, or social interaction.

It is estimated that there are 6,000,000 alcoholics plus an additional 4,000,000 or so problem drinkers in the U.S. This represents a significant number of our population. If each person with an alcohol problem directly affects the lives of a minimum of three other people, that produces a population of about 30,000,000 whose lives are directly affected by the drinking of another. An additional estimate of the significance of the problem is that approximately 5% to 7% of the national work force are active alcoholics. These numbers indicate the dramatic effect alcoholism has on our society. Though we don't know what causes alcoholism, the theories of causality abound: genetic predisposition, response to tension, etc. Research has not as yet provided us with the cause(s); however, it is known that people of all races, creeds, and socioeconomic levels make up the alcoholic population. Males and females are represented, as are all geographic regions of the United States and various religious groups.

Because of the progressive nature of the disease of alcoholism, it can be described in stages. In stage one, the alcoholic consumes alcohol to relieve tension, seeks more drinking occasions and drinks more frequently, changes drinking situations in an attempt to cover the increasing quantities of alcohol being consumed, and also changes friends to allow for greater consumption. The person begins to build tolerance to alcohol during this phase; that is, it takes increasing amounts of alcohol to receive the desired effect. The alcoholic is defensive about the amount of alcohol consumed and the number of drinking occasions. Denial of the fact that alcohol is playing an important role in the person's life often makes the person aggressively state, "I don't drink more than anyone else." As the person's life and lifestyle revolve around alcohol, family members are affected. The alcoholic may leave home, refuse to attend some functions where alcohol will not be served or where the desired amount can't be consumed, blame drinking episodes on other family members, and often not seem like the same person.

As the disease progresses to stage two, the alcoholic has difficulty keeping promises, experiences feelings of guilt and remorse because of drinking, and continues to blame others, while at the same time denying the problem. During this stage, the alcoholic requires larger amounts of alcohol, more frequently becomes intoxicated, and sneaks drinks. Sneaking drinks may not necessarily be a hidden bottle or supply. It may be having a few drinks before an event, or changing a day's pattern to drink at additional times such as lunch, or mid-afternoon, or on the way home from work. The alcoholic may also experience a blackout, which is a period of temporary amnesia. During this time, the alcoholic may have been functioning, but has no recollection of what occurred.

The alcoholic continues to rationalize his or her drinking during stage three and may lose control once drinking begins, that is, drinking to the point of intoxication with or without the desire to do so. The person may have more frequent black outs and continue to withdraw from family and friends. Withdrawal from responsibilities often occurs at this time, and problems at home or at work become visible. The person may begin morning drinking to settle queasiness or shakes. However, it is also possible that the person clings to denying the alcohol problem by the rationale of "I don't drink in the morning." This person may struggle through until a time set as being "acceptable" by him or her to drink. This time may or may not become progressively earlier. The alcoholic may choose another route for getting through the morning — minor tranquilizers. Since society often accepts the use of tranquilizers for many reasons, the alcoholic continues to deny the problem.

Alcoholics also rationalize that "I am not an alcoholic because I work." This rationale enables employee assistance programs to be successful. The job is put on the line, and the denial often cracks.

Daily patterns of behavior continue to revolve around alcoholism. Family members (spouse, children, siblings) frequently assume the consequences of the alcoholic's behavior (e.g., calling in sick for the person). Taking on some of the person's family responsibilities and chores are just some ways that this occurs. Keeping it to themselves, shutting themselves off from those who might suspect, attempting to make things right, and pretending that alcoholism is not present are other ways the family might deal with alcoholism. During stage four, the person has lost control over alcohol. When to drink, where to drink, and how much to drink, are governed only by the "to drink." Drinking has progressed to often or every day; morning drinking may be occurring as the person gives up the many rationalizations. Benders may be occurring, and the alcoholic will consume anything that will intoxicate him or her. At this time, a person either seeks help, goes under, or dies. The progression of the disease concept is complete.

This is not to imply that the disease of alcoholism must run its course. Intervention and treatment may occur at any point and the person may again lead a full and productive life. Since treatment is possible, the question of why so many people remain hidden by their families and friends and are allowed to progress through the stages of alcoholism is somewhat mystifying. One of the most important factors in why this is allowed to happen is that many people feel there is a stigma surrounding alcoholism. They incorrectly feel they can't or shouldn't share this problem with others, so they allow or cause it to become the family secret. This often creates many family problems, negatively impacts each family member, and delays the treatment necessary for the alcoholic. The sooner the treatment process begins, the better the person's chance of recovery and the family members' as well.

There are a variety of treatment services and facilities where an alcoholic can receive help (hospitals, inpatient or outpatient clinics, private facilities designed specifically for alcoholism treatment). An important source of help is Alcoholics Anonymous (A.A.) which is a nonsectarian, self-help fellowship for people who desire to stop drinking. A.A. has no membership list, no dues, and no constitution. Its aim is to provide an opportunity for alcoholics to become and remain sober. A.A. is listed in the telephone book and is accessible to all.

A tremendous source of help for family members is Al-Anon. Al-Anon family groups are patterned very closely after Alcoholics Anonymous. These groups function to help people who are close to the alcoholic with their problems during the time that the alcoholic is still drinking and also during sobriety.

Alateen groups were established for adolescent children of alcoholics to help these young people understand the disease of alcoholism and their alcoholic parent.

Other Drug Problems

Drug abuse has been defined to mean "the use of any drug to the point where it interferes with a person's health or with economic or social adjustment."[19] Drug dependence is "a state arising from repeated administration of a drug on a periodic or continuing basis. The characteristics of such a state will vary with the drug involved, and these characteristics must always be made clear by designating the particular type of drug dependence in each specific case; for example, drug dependence of morphine type, of amphetamine type, etc."[20] When we are discussing dependency on a drug, it must be understood that there are two separate elements for consideration. There may be a psychological dependence which may or may not include a physical dependence.

In case of psychological dependence, the user has a strong tendency to continue using a drug because of the pleasure it provides, or the user feels the drug is needed to alleviate discomfort. If the drug is discontinued, the person may feel anxious and tense but does not suffer severe physical discomfort. Many of us are psychologically dependent on a variety of drugs: coffee, cigarettes, soft drinks. Though excessive use of these substances may result in a health problem, we rarely think of these habits as drug problems.

However, physical dependence on a drug is more clearly thought of as a drug problem in our society. If a person is physically dependent upon a drug, withdrawal of the drug results in acute withdrawal symptoms (nausea, physical discomfort, and watery eyes and nose). The person exhibits an overwhelming desire to use the drug again as the maintenance of normal body functioning requires its use. This is the reason treatment programs begin with detoxification; that is, elimination of the drug from the body. This process may take anywhere from two to ten days. The person is usually medically monitored during this time to ease the withdrawal symptoms.

In terms of the drugs we've discussed, the following list from Lingeman's *Drugs From A to Z: A Dictionary* identifies those that produce psychic dependence.[21]

Drugs Producing Psychic Dependence But No Physical
  Dependence:
cocaine (no tolerance develops; severe depression and/or
  psychotic symptoms may accompany withdrawal after
  prolonged heavy use, motivating the resumption of use)

marijuana (insignificant tolerance develops)

hashish (some degree of tolerance may develop; some
degree of physical discomfort upon withdrawal after
prolonged use has been observed)

amphetamines (tolerance developes to a considerable
degree, but it is selective; i.e., insomnia and hyperexcit-
ability caused by the drug continue, while increasing
doses are necessary to sustain the drug's euphoriant
effects. If use has masked symptoms of fatigue, abrupt
withdrawal will often be accompanied by exhaustion and
severe depression and a strong temptation to return to
the drug.)

LSD (complete tolerance develops after only three days)

psilocybin (tolerance develops rapidly)

mescaline (tolerance develops rather slowly)

Drugs Producing Physical Dependence:

morphine type (tolerance develops to all actions, including
the lethal dose if the threatened intake is not carefully
regulated)

barbiturates, nonbarbiturate hypnotics, and sedatives;
minor tranquilizers (tolerance to the sedative effects, but
not the lethal dose, develops)

alcohol (some degree of tolerance develops; withdrawal
symptoms, such as delirium tremens, are similar to those
of barbiturates)

Tolerance is the cumulative resistance to the usual effects of
the drug. It is clear that in the case of drugs producing
physical dependence, psychological dependence may also be
present. Unfortunately, this separation of drugs into psychological but not physical dependence and physical dependence
should not put us at ease. Though users of physical
dependence-producing drugs suffer acute physical withdrawal
symptoms and perhaps also psychological ones, the psychological dependence-producing drugs may also have serious

consequences: preoccupation with the drug and drug taking, personality change, and lifestyle change.

People who are dependent on a drug or drugs often require treatment for their problem. Treatment facilities include hospitals, outpatient counseling, mental health centers, and residential programs specifically designed for chemically dependent people. There are also self-help groups which aid and support the dependent people (Pot Anonymous, Narcotics Anonymous, etc.). It is also important that family members of an addicted person realize they need support and help. Organizations to help the family are also available. To find out which ones are in your area, call your local hospital or mental health agency.

ENDNOTES

[1]L.D. Johnston, J. Bachman, and P. O'Malley, *Student Drug Use, Attitudes and Beliefs 1975-1982* (University of Michigan, Center for Social Research, 1982).

[2]"Sixteenth Annual Gallup Poll," *Phi Delta Kappan Magazine,* September 1984.

[3]R.A. Zucker and T.C. Harford, "National Study of the Demography of Adolescent Drinking Practices in 1980," *Journal of Studies on Alcohol* (November 1983).

[4]J.V. Rachel, S.A. Maisto, L.L. Guess, and R.L. Hubbard, "Alcohol Use Among Adolescents," *Fourth Special Report to the U.S. Congress on Alcohol and Health,* ed. by J. DeLuca, National Institute on Alcohol Abuse and Alcoholism under contract No. (ADM) 281-79-0022 (Washington, D.C., U.S. Government Printing Office, 1980).

[5]L. St. Clair Blackford, *Student Drug Use Surveys — San Mateo County, California, 1968-1975* (San Mateo County Department of Public Health and Welfare, 1975).

[6]Rachel, et. al., 1980.

[7]Report on 1983 Minnesota Survey on Drug Use and Related Attitudes, conducted by Peter Benson (Minneapolis, Minnesota, Search Institute, 1983).

[8]*Ibid.*

[9]Johnston, et. al., 1982.

[10]*Coping With Adolescent Substance Use,* ed. by R.J. Pandina (Rockville, Maryland, National Institute on Drug Abuse, 1978).

[11]J. Green, "Overview of Adolescent Drug Use," *Youth Drug Abuse: Problems, Issues and Treatment,* ed. by G.M. Beschner and A.S. Friedman (Lexington, Massachusetts, Lexington Books, 1979).

[12]*Demographic Trends and Drug Abuse, 1980-1995,* ed. by L.G. Richards (Rockville, Maryland, National Institute on Drug Abuse, 1981).

[13]R. Svendsen, T. Griffin, and D. McIntyre, *Chemical Health: School Athletics and Fine Arts Activities* (Center City, Minnesota, Hazelden Foundation, 1984).

[14]A.H. Maslow, *Toward a Psychology of Being,* Second Edition (New York, Van Nostrand Reinhold Co., 1968).

[15]R. Svendsen, et. al., 1984.

[16]T. Griffin and R. Svendsen, *The Student Assistance Program* (Center City, Minnesota, Hazelden Foundation, 1980).

[17]"Drug Dependence, Its Significance and Characteristics," *World Health Organization Bulletin* 32; 721-723, 1965.

[18]M. Keller, *The Definition of Alcoholism* (New Brunswick, New Jersey, Rutgers Center of Alcohol Studies, 1960).

[19]D.E. Smith and J. Luce, *Love Needs Care* (Boston, Massachusetts, Little, Brown and Co., 1971).

[20]Ibid.

[21]R.R. Lingeman, *Drugs from A to Z: A Dictionary,* Second Edition (New York, McGraw-Hill Book Co., 1974).

REFERENCES

Blackford, L. St. Clair, *Student Drug Use Surveys* — San Mateo County, California, 1968-1975, San Mateo County Department of Public Health and Welfare, 1975.

Coping with Adolescent Substance Use, ed. by R.J. Pandina, Rockville, Maryland, National Institute on Drug Abuse, 1978.

Demographic Trends and Drug Abuse, 1980-1995, ed. by L.G. Richards, Rockville, Maryland, National Institute on Drug Abuse, 1981.

Demone, H.W., Jr., "Drinking Attitudes and Practices of Male Adolescents," Ph.D. dissertation, Brandeis University, 1966 (University Microfilms No. 66-13637).

"Drug Dependence, Its Significance and Characteristics," *World Health Organization Bulletin* 32; 721-723, 1965.

Green, J. "Overview of Adolescent Drug Use," *Youth Drug Abuse: Problems, Issues and Treatment,* ed. by G.M. Beschner and A.S. Friedman, Lexington, Massachusetts, Lexington Books, 1979.

Griffin, T. and Svendsen, R., *The Student Assistance Program,* Center City, Minnesota, Hazelden Foundation, 1980. Available through Hazelden Educational Materials, order no. 1099.

Johnston, L.D., Bachman, J., and O'Malley, P., *Student Drug Use, Attitudes and Beliefs 1975-1982,* University of Michigan, Center for Social Research, 1982.

Keller, M., *The Definition of Alcoholism,* New Brunswick, New Jersey, Rutgers Center of Alcohol Studies, 1960.

Lingeman, R.R., *Drugs from A to Z: A Dictionary,* Second Edition, New York, McGraw-Hill Book Co., 1974. Available through Hazelden Educational Materials, order no. 4260.

Mandell, W., Cooper, A., Silberstein, R.M., Novick, J., and Koloski, E., *Youthful Drinking, New York State, 1962,*

Report to the Joint Legislative Committee on the Alcoholic
Beverage Control, Law of the New York State Legislature,
Staten Island, New York, 1963.

Maslow, A.H., *Toward a Psychology of Being,* Second Edition, New York, Van Nostrand Reinhold Co., 1968.

Milgram, G.G., *What, When, and How to Talk to Children About Alcohol and Other Drugs,* Center City, Minnesota, Hazelden Foundation, 1983. Available through Hazelden Educational Materials, order no. 1078.

Rachel, J.V., Maisto, S.A., Guess, L.L., and Hubbard, R.L., "Alcohol Use Among Adolescents," *Fourth Special Report to the U.S. Congress on Alcohol and Health,* ed. by J. Deluca, National Institute on Alcohol Abuse and Alcoholism under Contract No. (ADM) 281-79-0022, Washington, D.C., U.S. Government Printing Office, 1980.

Report on 1983 Minnesota Survey on Drug Use and Related Attitudes, conducted by Peter Benson, Minneapolis, Minnesota, Search Institute, 1983.

Smith, D.E., and Luce, J., *Love Needs Care,* Boston, Massachusetts, Little, Brown and Co., 1971.

Svendsen, R., Griffin, T., and McIntyre, D., *Chemical Health: School Athletics and Fine Arts Activities,* Center City, Minnesota, Hazelden Foundation, 1984.

Zucker, R.A. and Harford, T.C., "National Study of the Demography of Adolescent Drinking Practices in 1980," *Journal of Studies on Alcohol,* November 1983.

RESOURCES FOR ADDITIONAL INFORMATION

Alcoholics Anonymous World Services, Inc.
P.O. Box 459
Grand Central Station
New York, NY 10017

Al-Anon Family Group Headquarters
P.O. Box 182
Madison Square Station
New York, NY 10159

Addiction Research Foundation
33 Russell Street
Toronto, Ontario, M5S 2S1
Canada

Alcohol and Drug Problems Association of
   North America (ADPA)
444 North Capitol Street NW, Suite 181
Washington, DC 20001

American Medical Association
535 N. Dearborn Street
Chicago, IL 60610

Hazelden Educational Materials
P.O. Box 176, Pleasant Valley Road
Center City, MN 55012

National Clearinghouse for Alcohol Information
P.O. Box 2345, Dept. 10
Rockville, MD 20852

National Congress of Parents and Teachers
700 North Rush Street
Chicago, IL 60611

National Council on Alcoholism, Inc.
733 3rd Avenue, 14th Floor
New York, NY 10017

National Institute on Alcohol Abuse and
  Alcoholism (NIAAA)
5600 Fishers Lane
Rockville, MD 20852

National Institute on Drug Abuse
11400 Rockville Pike
Rockville, MD 20852

North Conway Institute
14 Beacon Street Room 715
Boston, MA 02108

Rutgers Center of Alcohol Studies
P.O. Box 969
Piscataway, NJ 08854

Divisions of Alcoholism and Drug Abuse,
Departments of Education, Mental Health, and Safety
Councils of various states also may have alcohol and
drug information available for distribution.

Hazelden

Other titles that will interest you...

What, When, and How to Talk to Children About Alcohol and Other Drugs: A Guide for Parents
by Gail Gleason Milgram, Ed.D.
   Written for today's parents who grew up in "another world," this book provides the framework, information, and communication skills parents need to discuss alcohol and other drugs with their children. (98 pp.)
Order No. 1078A

Never Too Early
Never Too Late
   An excellent resource for parents and others concerned about alcohol and other drug problems. Why do people misuse alcohol and other drugs? What contributes to misuse? What are the warning signs of misuse? Where can families find help? These topics and more are explored under the premise that drug education begins with parents. (20 pp.)
Order No. 1391B

Kids, Drugs, and the Law
by David G. Evans, Esq.
   Can a minor consent to chemical dependency treatment? Are parents liable for their children's private or civil misdeeds? Attorney and author David G. Evans answers these questions and more. This highly informative book will help parents understand the legal rights and responsibilities of kids who use alcohol and other drugs. (88 pp.)
Order No. 1341A

For price and order information, please call one of our Customer Service Representatives.

Hazelden
Educational Materials

Pleasant Valley Road
Box 176
Center City, MN 55012-0176

(800) 328-9000
(Toll Free. U.S. Only.)
(800) 328-0500
(Toll Free. Film and Video Orders)
(800) 257-0070
(Toll Free. MN Only)
(612) 257-4010
(MN, AK, & Outside U.S.)